feast of eden

RECIPES FROM CALIFORNIA'S GARDEN PARADISE

D0619421

The Junior League of Monterey County

Design: Kathryn B. Stark
Editorial: Joann Vaughan
Photography: Douglas
                    Sandberg

Published by The Junior League of Monterey County, Incorporated
P.O. Box 2291
Monterey, CA 93942-2291

Since 1963, The Junior League of Monterey County has made a permanent, positive impact in our community through our trained leadership and successful projects. Today, the Junior League commitment to Monterey County continues through our Scholarship program, our Community Grants program, and our projects dealing with teenage mothers, health care and children's education. Proceeds from the sale of *Feast of Eden* will contribute to the establishment of an interactive children's museum in Monterey County.

ISBN 0-9637963-0-5

Printed in the United States of America by Wimmer Brothers Memphis, Tennessee

Contents

Introduction

Where the Santa Lucia Mountains separate the fields of Salinas from the Pacific Ocean, lies the garden paradise of Monterey County, California. Here is a style of casual elegance. There is presentation without pretense, polish without posturing, and an attitude of relaxed refinement.

Life in Monterey County is highly textured. From the rocky cliffs and towering redwoods of the Big Sur Coast, to the rich loam of the agricultural fields of Salinas, to the thatched roofs of story book Carmel, to the diamond sparkle of the aquamarine waters of Pebble Beach. Life is meant to be touched, felt, experienced. And food, fresh from the fields or the sea, is a great part of that experience.

Fishing boats unload their catch daily at Monterey harbor. Lettuce, broccoli, strawberries, tomatoes, and more are harvested in the Salinas Valley, artichokes in Carmel and Castroville. Cattle graze along the coastal ranches. Inland, away from the fog, fruit orchards and berry vines thrive, while a bounteous grape crop enables the local vineyards to produce world renowned wines.

The richness of Monterey County's abundant harvest is combined in the kitchen to produce meals that are subtly sophisticated, make the opulent ordinary, and are elegant enough for everyday.

The Junior League of Monterey County is proud to be part of the tapestry of our community. The Junior League brings together over 500 women from all areas of Monterey County who are committed to the idea that our community can and will be improved through the effective actions of women who care. Commitment, caring, community–these three words are basic to our purpose and our action.

We are pleased to bring to you this collection of California cooking that combines the freshest of ingredients for the most favorable of outcomes.

So sit back and relax, imagine the sun setting over the Pacific Ocean and savor the flavors of "Feast of Eden".

FESTIVE FEASTS

Carmel Bach Festival
Elegant Dinner

PAPAYA WITH BAY SHRIMP, *page 13*

VEAL ROLLS DEL MONTE, *page 185*

ROSEMARY GLAZED CARROTS, *page 85*

SAVORY GREEN BEANS WITH SHALLOTS, *page 103*

· FESTIVE GREENS AND CITRUS SALAD, *page 60*

WHITE CHOCOLATE CREME BRULEE , *page 230*

The Carmel Bach Festival today is the mature form of the infant musical offering created by Dene Denney and Hazel Watrous, two women dedicated to enhancing the cultural life of the Monterey Peninsula. It all began in 1935 as a three-day concert at the Sunset School Auditorium and at the Carmel Mission Basilica. It has grown to become a three week festival of performances by international artists, encompassing concerts, opera, recitals, master classes, lieder programs, lectures, symposia, and educational programs. The festival continues its original mission-to celebrate the works of Johann Sebastian Bach, his contemporaries, and his musical heirs.

Pebble Beach Concours d'Elegance Sumptuous Picnic

More than forty years ago, the Pebble Beach Concours D'Elegance was a mere adjunct to the Pebble Beach Road Race, held on the roads of Del Monte Forest from 1950-1956. Since that time, it has become the finest antique car show in the world, attracting such celebrity auto enthusiasts as Bob Hope, Clint Eastwood, Jackie Stewart, Jay Leno and Ralph Lauren.

More than 140 of the most spectacular automobiles known to the industry are exhibited on the lawns of The Lodge at Pebble Beach, overlooking the 18th green. Many of these grand touring cars date back to the turn of the century and boast innovations revolutionary for their time. Spectators are invited to picnic on the lawn and delight in the most extraordinary cars the world has to offer.

Pebble Beach AT&T National Pro-Am Clambake

CLAMBAKE CHOWDER, *page 47*
CRISPY POTATO CHICKEN, *page 191*
BASMATI RICE WITH ARUGULA SALAD, *page 78*
MARINATED BABY ASPARAGUS, *page 89*
ZUCCHINI TOMATO FOCACCIA BREAD, *page 128*
FRESH APPLE CAKE, *page 240*

In 1937, Bing Crosby invited a group of friends to get together for a round of golf and a "clambake" at Rancho Santa Fe in Southern California. That first gathering of Hollywood celebrities and golf greats gave birth to the Bing Crosby Pro-Am, with Sam Snead taking the top prize of $500.

The tournament made its home at Pebble Beach in 1946 after a local newspaper reporter, Ted Durein, came up with the idea of attracting more tourists to the area with a major special event.

In 1985 the AT&T Company became the sponsor of the event. The Crosby name was withdrawn at the family's request.

The AT&T Pebble Beach National Pro-Am now hosts a field of 360 golf professionals and amateurs split evenly. Professionals compete for a $1.25 million purse. The tournament has raised well over $11 million for over 150 nonprofit charitable organizations since its inception. The majority of the tournament proceeds are donated to the Youth Fund set up by Bing Crosby which channels funds into youth-oriented charities and scholarships.

Monterey Wine Festival Wine Tasting Cocktail Party

TOMATO & BACON BRUSCHETTA, *page 23*
EGGPLANT BRUSCHETTA, *page 22*
SALMON MOUSSE WITH
SOUR CREAM DILL SAUCE, *page 135*
BAKED STUFFED OYSTER TRIO, *page 17*
MONTEREY PHYLLO TRIANGLES, *page 29*
CYPRESS CHEESE TART, *page 27*

The Monterey Wine Festival is celebrating its 18th year as the nation's original and most lavish wine festival highlighting the finest wines from California. Every March more than 200 vintners feature over 800 different bottlings from California's various wine-making regions. Successful from the beginning, The Monterey Wine Festival outgrew its initial sites by 1980 and moved to its present location, The Monterey Conference Center. The festival continues to attract standing-room-only crowds, drawn by the combination of world class wine and food tastings; seminars by industry leaders such as Brooks Firestone, Robert Mondavi and Peter Sichel; and celebrity guest speakers including Wayne Rogers, Burgess Meredith, Jacques Pepin, Wolfgang Puck and Julia Child.

The Wine Auction, formed as a nonprofit organization, finances scholarships in the fields of viticulture, oenology and hotel and restaurant administration.

❦

Salinas Valley Rodeo
Barbecue

RED & YELLOW PEPPER SOUP, *page 38*
CAESAR SALAD WITH HEART, *page 56*
SMOKED JALAPENO GAME HENS, *page 200*
BLACK BEANS CILANTRO, *page 101*
SEA & VALLEY BROCCOLI, *page 87*
OLLALIEBERRY COBBLER , *page 222*

Salinas tradition at its best, the California Rodeo has attracted top cowboys and cowgirls from around the country since its beginning in 1911. With its cowboy contests, races, and horse shows, Rodeo Week passes down a tradition in the truest sense of the word by bringing the Old West back to life for all to enjoy.

The nonprofit self-supporting California Rodeo is one of the richest four-day performance events of its kind in the world. Each year the California Rodeo Association passes along its proceeds to local service clubs, schools and charities. As the largest event held in Salinas, the Rodeo's economic impact to the community is over $16 million per year.

Old Whaling Station
Wedding Luncheon

ARTICHOKE PHYLLO FLOWERS, *page 11*
SALMON WITH TOMATO,
CUCUMBER & BASIL, *page 136*
WEDDING SALAD, *page 52*
BRAISED CELERY WITH WALNUTS, *page 90*
CREAM CHEESE POUND CAKE
WITH BLUEBERRY SAUCE, *page 245*

The perfect marriage of Monterey's past and future can be found at the Old Whaling Station, an historic adobe located near Fisherman's Wharf in Heritage Harbor. Built in 1848 by Scottish adventurer David Wright, the building and grounds combine the charms of a Scottish cottage with the unique texture of Spanish adobe.

Unlike other Monterey adobes, built in Mexican fashion to face the rising sun, the home was built with a view of Monterey Bay. After Wright left to seek his fortune in the California gold fields, the building was used as the head-quarters of the Old Monterey Bay Whaling Company. Portuguese whalers, sighting the migrating whales from the upstairs, would race to climb into small eight-man boats to hunt whales with hand-thrown harpoons.

The Junior League of Monterey County leased the building in 1979 from the state of California and began restoration. The historic house is one of the few of the city's original buildings that can be enjoyed by the public. The home can be enjoyed for the day - for a wedding, reception or special party. For rental information, please contact the Junior League of Monterey County, 408-375-5356.

APPETIZERS & SOUPS

Pebble Beach

There are many places the rich and famous visit; there are few where they live. In Pebble Beach pretense is put aside and prominent people are just the folks next door. Neighbors meet perusing arugula at the market, trading recipes on the golf course, and entertaining in their homes. At twilight, the orange sun sets in a sapphire sky over a purple ocean, bringing the end of the day, and the dawn of the evening – a time to relax and enjoy the great beginnings to a great meal.

Artichoke Phyllo Flowers

9 sheets phyllo pastry, thawed

6 to 8 tablespoons butter, melted

1 9-ounce package frozen artichoke hearts, thawed and diced

2 tablespoons butter

2 shallots, minced

2 cloves garlic, minced or pressed

8 ounces Ricotta cheese

1 egg, beaten

1/2 cup half and half

1/2 cup grated Parmesan cheese

2 tablespoons snipped chives

salt and pepper

To make filling in an 8 to 10 inch frying pan, melt butter over medium to high heat. Saute shallots for 1 minute. Add diced artichokes and saute for 5 to 6 minutes or until lightly browned, adding the garlic the last 2 minutes. Set aside to cool. In a bowl soften the ricotta, then beat in the egg and half and half until blended. Add the Parmesan cheese, chives and artichoke mixture. Salt and pepper to taste and mix well.

To assemble: Lay 1 sheet of phyllo dough on a flat surface and lightly brush with melted butter. Repeat 2 more times. Cut into 5 strips lengthwise and 4 strips widthwise to make 20 3 inch squares. Lay one square on a work surface and place another square on top of it at opposite angles. Press the squares into a cup of a mini muffin pan. Repeat until all cups are filled with phyllo squares. Spoon filling equally into cups. Bake at 350° for 15 to 20 minutes or until filling feels set and phyllo is lightly golden. Cool 5 minutes. Gently ease out of pan with tip of knife.

Zesty Crab and Artichoke Dip

Pita Triangles

8 large pita loaves

1/2 cup unsalted butter

Cut each pita loaf into eight wedges and separate each wedge into two triangles. Arrange the triangles roughside up in one layer on cookie sheet. Brush lightly with butter and season with salt. Bake the triangles in the upper third of a 375° oven for 10 to 12 minutes. The triangles may be made one day in advance and kept in an airtight container.

1 large green bell pepper chopped

1 tablespoon vegetable oil

2 14-ounce cans artichoke hearts, drained and chopped fine

2 cups mayonnaise

1/2 cup thinly sliced scallions

1/2 cup drained and chopped, bottled pimento or roasted red pepper

1 cup freshly grated Parmesan cheese

1-1/2 tablespoons fresh lemon juice

4 teaspoons worcestershire sauce

3 pickled jalapeno peppers, seeded and minced

1 teaspoon celery salt

1 pound crab meat, picked over

1/3 cup sliced almonds, toasted lightly

In small skillet, cook the bell pepper in oil over moderate heat, stir until soft. Let cool. In large bowl combine bell pepper with next ten ingredients. Stir in crab meat gently. Transfer the mixture to a buttered baking dish, Sprinkle with almonds. The dip may be prepared up to one day in advance to this point and kept chilled. Bake the dip in a preheated 375° oven for 25 to 30 minutes or until golden and bubbly. Serve with pita triangles.

7th Hole,
Pebble Beach
Golf Links

Crispy Potato Chicken

Tournament
Gallery,
Spyglass Hill
Golf Course

*A Concours
d'Elegance Picnic*

Pesto Lamb d'Elegance

*A "classic",
Pebble Beach
Concours
d'Elegance*

Old Whaling Station, Monterey

Wedding Spinach Salad with Yogurt Dressing

Wedding in the Old Whaling Station Garden

Salinas California Rodeo

Red & Yellow Roasted Pepper Soup

Fresh vegetables from the Salinas Valley

Papaya with Bay Shrimp

3/4 pound bay shrimp
3 tablespoons lemon juice
2 tablespoons
  Dijon mustard
1/2 cup salad oil
2 papayas
Freshly ground black
  pepper to taste
Butter lettuce leaves

Rinse the shrimp in cold water. Combine the lemon juice, mustard and salad oil together and marinate the shrimp in this mixture for at least two hours.

Peel the papayas and cut in two. Arrange either in halves or in a fan shape over butter lettuce leaves. Divide the shrimp mixture over the papayas and add freshly ground pepper.

Artichokes and Prawns with Tarragon Vinaigrette

Craig Ling
The Restaurant at Mission Ranch

Known for its fine food and home town atmosphere as much as for its famous owner, Clint Eastwood, The Mission Ranch is a local favorite. A tradition since 1882, The Mission Ranch rests peacefully on acreage with views of meadows and wetlands to the south, and across to Carmel River Beach and rocky Point Lobos.

Adjacent to Carmel Mission, the second oldest mission in California, the Ranch was originally a dairy. The present dining room was the creamery and the "Barn" was the old cow barn. In its present form, the Restaurant has preserved the flavor of its historic past.

2 lemons, cut in half
1 gallon cold water
1 teaspoon salt
4 medium artichokes
4 sprigs fresh tarragon, leaves picked and coarsely chopped or 4 teaspoons dried
1/2 cup white wine or beer
8 large prawns in the shell, or any amount you would like to serve

crushed chilies and celery salt or seafood seasoning to taste

Tarragon Vinaigrette
1/3 cup red wine vinegar
2 egg yolks
1 cup olive oil
salt and pepper to taste
1 bunch parsley, finely chopped

Squeeze juice from half a lemon into one gallon cold water, add salt and set aside. With a sharp knife cut the top third off the artichokes, with scissors trim top off remaining leaves at the bottom so no fingers will get pricked. Then cut the stem at the base of the artichoke, rub with lemon and place in cold water. After trimming all the artichokes pour off excess water leaving just enough to cover, cut each artichoke in half lengthwise and return to water with stems and 1/4 of the chopped tarragon leaves. Place on medium heat until cooked through. The artichokes are done when the base is easily pierced with a knife; about the consistency of cool butter. This should take about 15 to 20 minutes; do not cook too fast. Carefully remove choke from each artichoke half and discard.

(Continued on next page)

Pour wine or beer in the bottom of a pan for steaming and bring to a boil. Place prawns in pan and sprinkle with liberal amount of seafood seasoning or crushed chilies and celery salt, cover and steam until cooked. Stir or shake pan once or twice; this should take about 4 to 6 minutes.

To prepare tarragon vinaigrette place half the red wine vinegar and the egg yolks in an electric mixing bowl. The bowl and oil should not be cold; room temperature or slightly warm is best. With bowl on medium high pour oil in slow steady stream. Stopping the oil to let it mix is fine but putting too much in will separate or break the vinaigrette. The oil will make a mayonnaise; thin by adding a squeeze of lemon and as much of the remaining vinegar as you prefer. Season with salt and pepper and add the chopped parsley and remaining tarragon.

Place each artichoke half on individual plate, drizzle with vinaigrette and place a shelled prawn in scooped choke area.

Serves eight.

Poached Shrimp with Fennel Aioli

Aioli

2 medium fennel bulbs
1 1/2 cups plus 3
     tablespoons olive oil
1 1/2 teaspoons
     fennel seeds
1 1/2 tablespoons white
     wine vinegar
3 garlic cloves, chopped
3 egg yolks
white pepper

Shrimp

2 teaspoons fennel seeds
2 cups white wine
2 1/2 pounds uncooked
     medium shrimp,
     peeled, deveined, tails
     intact
8 cups water
red and green bell
     pepper strips

For Aioli: Cut stalks and fronds off fennel bulbs, reserve for garnish. Chop bulbs, heat 3 tablespoons oil in large skillet over medium heat. Add chopped fennel, fennel seeds, and vinegar. Saute 10 minutes, stirring frequently. Add 1 1/2 garlic cloves and remaining 1 1/2 cups olive oil. Reduce heat to low, cover and cook until fennel is tender, about 35 minutes. Place remaining 1 1/2 garlic cloves and yolks in blender. Add hot fennel, using slotted spoon. Process until smooth. Gradually add oil from fennel mixture in slow steady stream. Process until emulsified, season with white pepper. Return to skillet, heat thoroughly, whisking constantly, cover and chill. Can be done up to two days ahead.

For Shrimp: Bring water, wine, fennel to boil; add shrimp, simmer until shrimp are opaque, about 2 minutes. Drain. Rinse with cold water. Arrange on platter with pepper strips; with fennel aioli in bowl in center. Garnish with fennel fronds.

Baked Stuffed Oyster Trio

Maria Anderson
Sandbar & Grill

24 oysters shucked, on
the half shell

1/2 cup blue cheese
crumbles
1 teaspoon chopped
garlic

1/4 cup chopped
artichoke hearts
1/4 cup shredded
Cheddar cheese
2 tablespoons vinaigrette
dressing

1/4 cup bacon bits
1/4 cup chopped onions
1/4 cup chopped red
and green peppers
1/4 cup finely chopped
jalapeno pepper
1/4 cup seasoned
breadcrumbs
1/4 cup Parmesan cheese

3/4 cup seasoned
breadcrumbs

Mix each set of ingredients separately. Add 1/4 cup
seasoned breadcrumbs to each set, to tighten mixture.
Spread open oysters in half shell on baking sheet (discard
the half without the meat). Evenly distribute mixture into
each oyster half shell. Top the spicy bacon oysters with
grated parmesan. Bake at 350° for 12 minutes.

Caviar Cucumber Torta

Sour Cream Layer
2 packages unflavored
   gelatin
1/2 cup water
1 cup sour cream
1/2 cup plain yogurt
3/4 cup chopped
   red onion

Cucumber Layer
1 1/2 english cucumber
   or seedless hothouse
   cucumber, coarsely
   chopped
2 tablespoons lemon juice

3 tablespoons mayonnaise
dash hot sauce
8 small green onions,
   chopped

Egg Layer
4 hard boiled eggs
1/2 cup mayonnaise
1/4 cup finely
   chopped parsley
3/4 teaspoon salt
dash hot sauce
1 3 1/2-ounce jar
   black or red caviar
fresh lemon juice

To prepare sour cream layer dissolve gelatin in water, add other ingredients. Pour into 2 quart souffle pan and chill to set.

To prepare cucumber layer puree 1/2 cucumber with mayonnaise, lemon juice, green onions, and hot sauce. Combine puree with remaining cucumber and 2 tablespoons gelatin. Gently spread over sour cream layer and chill to set.

To make egg layer combine all ingredients with 1 tablespoon of gelatin. Neatly spread egg mixture over cucumber layer. Cover dish tightly with plastic wrap and refrigerate overnight. Just before serving, place caviar in fine sieve and rinse gently under cold running water. Sprinkle with lemon juice. Drain. Remove from mold by loosening edges and turn upside down. Spread caviar over top. Serve with crackers.

Salmon Mousse and Sour Cream Dill Sauce

Salmon Mousse

2 cups of salmon (cooked or canned)

2/3 cup evaporated milk

2 cups soft bread crumbs

1 egg, well beaten

3 tablespoons minced onion

1/2 teaspoon salt

1/4 teaspoon poultry seasoning

Sour Cream Dill Sauce

1 egg

1 teaspoon salt

1 teaspoon pepper

pinch of sugar

4 teaspoons lemon juice

1 teaspoon finely chopped onion

2 tablespoons finely cut dill

1 1/2 cups sour cream

To prepare salmon loaf mix salmon, milk and bread crumbs together until well blended. Add beaten egg, onion, seasoning and mix. Press the mixture into a greased loaf pan. Bake about 40 minutes at 350°. Serve with Sour Cream Dill Sauce.

To prepare sour cream dill sauce beat egg until lemon color. Add the next 5 ingredients. Mix well. Blend in the dill and sour cream. Serve on Salmon Mousse.

Mushrooms del Mar

For a different idea drop an escargot into a mushroom cap add a dab of garlic and butter. Bake for 10 minutes at 350° or until butter is bubbling. Enjoy this easy and different appetizer.

12 large mushroom caps
4 tablespoons butter
1 green onion, chopped
24 bay scallops
1/2 cup crab meat
1/3 cup grated
    Parmesan cheese
salt and pepper, to taste

Saute all ingredients except mushrooms and cheese, for about 2 minutes. Lay mushroom caps in baking dish. Stuff sauteed mixture evenly into each cap. Sprinkle with parmesan cheese. Bake 350° for 10 minutes.

Mushrooms Tuscany

2 Italian sweet sausages
1/4 cup finely
    minced onion
1 garlic clove, peeled
    and crushed
olive oil, if necessary
1/4 cup fresh
    chopped parsley
1/4 cup chopped
    black olives
1/3 cup white sauce
12 large white
    mushrooms
Parmesan cheese

White Sauce
1 tablespoons butter
1 1/2 tablespoons flour
1/2 cup milk
salt and pepper to taste

Remove sausage from casings and crumble into skillet. Saute, stirring often until meat is cooked thoroughly. Remove sausage, leaving fat in skillet.

Saute onions and garlic in rendered fat until soft and golden - use a little olive oil if needed. Stir in parsley and add to sausage meat. Stir olives and white sauce into sausage mixture, combining thoroughly. Season with salt and pepper   Take stems off mushrooms. Wash carefully and lightly salt and pepper. Fill each mushroom cap with the sausage mixture. Place caps in lightly greased baking dish. Sprinkle with Parmesan cheese. Bake at 450° for 15 minutes until well browned. Cool 5 minutes.

Eggplant Bruschetta

1 eggplant, peeled and
   diced
1/2 teaspoon salt
2 tablespoons olive oil
1 tablespoon minced
   garlic
1 tablespoon dried basil,
   crumbled
pepper to taste
1/3 cup pesto
1 baguette, sliced and
   browned
2 ounces grated
   Provolone cheese
2 ounces crumbled
   Gorgonzola cheese

Place peeled and diced eggplant in colander, sprinkle with salt. Let stand 30 minutes and pat dry with paper towels. Heat oil in skillet over medium high heat. Add eggplant, garlic and basil. Saute 8 to 10 minutes until lightly browned. Season with pepper. Spread 1 teaspoon pesto on each slice of bread. Top with about 1 tablespoon of each - eggplant, Provolone, and Gorgonzola. Place on cookie sheets and broil 3 to 4 minutes until cheese is melted. Serve warm.

Tomato and Bacon Bruschetta

24 1/2-inch thick slices
   French bread, lightly
   browned on each side.
1/3 cup chopped green
   onions
2 teaspoons minced garlic
1 1/2 cup chopped
   tomatoes, peeled and
   seeded
1/4 cup chicken stock
1/4 teaspoon red pepper
   flakes
6 strips of bacon, cooked
   and crumbled
3 tablespoons olive oil

Brown French bread in a 350° oven 3 to 5 minutes per side. Heat oil in skillet over medium to high heat. Saute onions 2 minutes. Add garlic and saute 1 minute. Mix in tomatoes, stock and pepper flakes. Cook 10 minutes until liquid evaporates. Can be prepared 1 day ahead and refrigerated. Spread tomato mixture on bread slices, sprinkle with bacon. Bake at 350° for 8 minutes.

Chicken Pesto Pinwheels

*P*ebble Beach's most famous roadway, the Seventeen Mile Drive isn't 17 miles long.

The drive along the ocean got its name long before Pebble Beach was ever developed. Guests staying at the posh Hotel Del Monte in Monterey often went for recreational drives along the ocean. On a day's outing from the hotel, visitors would take a dirt road that wound 17 miles through Monterey, Pacific Grove and into Del Monte Forest. A pine lodge, forerunner to the Lodge at Pebble Beach, was opened in 1909 as a watering hole for the day visitors.

2 whole chicken breasts,
　　skinned and boned
1/2 cup pesto sauce
2 tablespoons plain
　　yogurt
2 tablespoons butter

Pound chicken breasts to 1/4 inch thickness. Combine pesto sauce and yogurt. Spread pesto mixture on chicken and roll up. Secure with toothpicks. Melt butter in skillet over medium heat. Brown chicken on all sides. Place chicken in a baking dish and bake 20 minutes at 350°. Chill and slice into pinwheels. Serve at room temperature.

Pesto Cheesecake

1 3-inch wheel of Brie or
    Camembert cheese
2 medium cloves of garlic,
    peeled
1/4 cup pine nuts
1/3 cup fresh basil leaves
9 sundried tomatoes,
    jarred in oil
1 baguette

Cut wheel of cheese horizontally in half. In food processor combine garlic, pine nuts, basil and sundried tomatoes. Blend. Spread mixture on cheese. Microwave for 45 seconds. Spread onto sliced baguettes or water crackers.

On Washington's Birthday, 1919, Samuel F. B. Morse opened the Lodge at Pebble Beach, the hotel symbolizing his philosophy - that guests should be well entertained and well maintained.

The rich and famous were already accustomed to vacationing on the Monterey Peninsula at the Hotel Del Monte and soon they flocked to S.F.B. Morse's new resort - and to the newly finished Pebble Beach Golf Links. From the beginning, Pebble Beach was an exclusive retreat for presidents and princes, celebrities and athletes, industrialists and statesmen. Charles Lindberg, Erroll Flynn, Bette Davis, Sinclair Lewis, Salvador Dali, Ringo Starr, Gerald Ford, John F. Kennedy, to name a few all relaxed in the upscale atmosphere of the Lodge at Pebble Beach. Glenn Ford and Anne Baxter filmed Follow the Sun there, the story of Ben Hogan. With nature's help, Morse had created the finest golfing resort in the world.

Roasted Garlic and Gorgonzola Quesadilla

Fresh Basil Salsa

2 cups peeled, chopped,
  seeded cucumber
1 1/2 cups coarsely
  chopped fresh basil
Finely grated zest
  of 1 lemon
Freshly ground black
  pepper
2 tablespoons fresh
  lemon juice

Mix in bowl. Fifteen minutes before serving, toss with lemon juice. Mix well.

1 large head garlic
2 tablespoons olive oil
10 flour tortillas
4 ounces Gorgonzola
  cheese
fresh salsa
salt and pepper, to taste

Preheat oven to 350°. Cut off top point of garlic bulb and tips of side, just enough to reveal clove inside pocket. Brush with olive oil. Bake for 45 minutes at 350°. Cool. Spread a clove of roasted garlic on tortilla. Crumble cheese on tortilla, fold in half. Cook in ungreased pan until light brown on each side. Cut into triangles and serve immediately with salsa.

Cypress Cheese Tart

Crust
1 1/2 cups flour
1/8 pound butter
4 egg yolks
1/4 cup grated
   Parmesan cheese
1/8 teaspoon salt
1/8 teaspoon cayenne
1/8 teaspoon dry mustard
1/4 cup milk
1 egg white

Filling
1/4 cup butter
10 eggs
1/2 cup flour
1 teaspoon baking
   powder
1/8 teaspoon salt
8 ounces diced green
   chilies
1 teaspoon cayenne
15 ounces Ricotta cheese
1 pound Monterey
   Jack cheese

Pastry: Place flour in bowl, or food processor. Add butter, egg yolks, cheese, salt, cayenne, mustard. Mix until smooth. Add enough milk to make dough gather into ball. Roll out on floured surface. Place in an 8-inch pie or quiche pan. Paint surface with egg white.

Filling: Melt butter over low heat. Mix all ingredients together. Pour into shells. Bake at 350° for 45 minutes. Cool, cut into small slices.

He was called the "Duke of Del Monte" and he built Pebble Beach.

Samuel F.B. Morse was named for his famous great uncle who perfected the telegraph, and he, too, aspired to greatness.

An Eastern gentleman by breeding, Morse captained the 1906 Yale football team. At Yale, he met Templeton Crocker, nephew of railroad and banking baron William Crocker. It was Crocker who brought Morse to the West.

Fabulous Brie in Pastry

*S*amuel F. B. Morse was hired by William Crocker to manage the "Del Monte unit", part of the Pacific Improvement Company - the company that owned the famous Hotel Del Monte with all its amenities and a vacant 5300 acre tract of land known as the Del Monte Forest. Morse was 29.

Morse believed that guests should first be entertained - room and board was secondary. He first set out to improve the ambiance of the hotel. He redecorated the hotel, returned polo to the fields, restored smoking in the dining room and dancing in the lounge, and totally revitalized the golf course - replacing the original sand greens with modern greens of grass watered with an installed sprinkler system.

❦

1 sheet puff pastry or
   make your own
   (see below)
1/3 cup crumbled
   blue cheese
1 10 ounce wheel of Brie
1/4 cup apricot jam
sesame seeds
1 egg, beaten

Slice Brie wheel in half across the round, so you end up with two circles. Spoon on apricot jam and then crumbled blue cheese. Place top of wheel back on top. Wrap cheese in rolled out pastry sheet, sealing all edges and tucking underneath. Brush with beaten egg and sprinkle with sesame seeds. Bake for 30 minutes or until golden brown.

You can use left-over tidbits of pastry to make leaves and designs on top of the pastry covered ball. Recipe taste can be changed by substituting chutney for the apricot jam.

Demi Puff Pastry
2 1/2 cups flour, sifted
1 teaspoon salt
1 large egg
2 tablespoons milk
1 cup butter

Blend flour, butter and salt in food processor or bowl with mixer. Add egg and milk while still blending. Finish kneading by hand or in processor until mixture forms a ball. Chill for 1 hour. Roll into large circle and continue with recipe.

❦

Monterey Phyllo Triangles

1 pound phyllo dough,
   defrosted
1 1/2 to 2 cups melted
   butter
1 pound Monterey Jack
   cheese, grated
2 bunches parsley, finely
   minced
2 eggs, beaten
3 to 4 cloves garlic,
   minced
salt and pepper

Samuel F. B. Morse had seen Pebble Beach and envisioned what could be built there. Hired to liquidate the "Del Monte Unit", he instead put together a deal to buy the original Hotel Del Monte and grounds, and all other properties - including the vacant Pebble Beach land.

In 1919, at the age of 33, Morse bought the whole package for $1.5 million.

To make filling combine grated cheese and parsley in bowl. Add garlic to beaten eggs and toss with cheese mixture to moisten. Salt and pepper to taste.

To assemble: Remove phyllo dough from package and immediately put between sheets of wax paper or plastic wrap and a moist towel to keep from drying out. Lay one sheet of phyllo dough on a flat surface and lightly brush with melted butter. Working quickly, lay another sheet of phyllo on top and brush with butter. Repeat once more to make three layers. With a sharp knife, cut the sheets into about 6 or 7-inch by 2 1/2 inch strips width-wise. Spoon about 1 teaspoon of the filling onto the lower edge of each phyllo strip. Fold edge of dough over filling to form a triangle. Continue folding triangles as you fold a flag until you reach the top of the strip. Brush finished triangles with butter to secure edges.

Place on cookie sheet and bake at 425° for 10 to 12 minutes or until lightly golden. May be frozen if making in advance.

Polenta Roma

2 1/2 cups water
1 teaspoon Italian
   seasoning
3/4 cup polenta
1 tablespoon oil
1/2 cup Parmesan cheese
1 tablespoon minced
   parsley
1/8 cup finely chopped
   sun dried tomatoes
1/8 cup finely chopped
   artichoke hearts
2 tablespoons finely
   chopped black olives

In double boiler, bring water to a boil; add seasonings. Slowly add polenta stirring constantly. Let bubble for 2 to 3 minutes while stirring. Let simmer, covered, for 20 to 25 minutes. Stir in fresh parsley, oil, Parmesan, sun-dried tomatoes, artichoke hearts, and black olives. Press into a lightly oiled 8x9 inch glass pan and let cool 3 to 4 hours.

To serve, reheat topped with marinara sauce. Will keep in refrigerator for several days. Freezes well.

Creamy Polenta with Roasted Wild Mushrooms

Polenta

1 3/4 cup water
1 3/4 cup chicken stock
1 teaspoon minced garlic
3/4 cup polenta
2/3 cup creme fraiche or
sour cream
1/4 cup grated Monterey
Jack cheese
1/4 cup grated
Parmesan cheese
3 tablespoons butter

Roasted Wild Mushrooms

8 garlic cloves,
thinly sliced
3 tablespoons olive oil
3 tablespoons balsamic
vinegar or red
wine vinegar
3 fresh rosemary sprigs or
1 teaspoon dried
3 fresh thyme sprigs or
1 teaspoon dried
4 cups fresh wild mush
rooms (such as
shitake or cremine)

Creme Fraiche

1 cup whipping cream
1 cup sour cream
Whisk together. Cover with plastic wrap and let stand in warm place for 24 hours. Whisk again. Cover and refrigerate until chilled. Will keep up to 2 weeks.

Polenta: Preheat oven to 350°.   Bring water, chicken stock, and minced garlic to boil in ovenproof saucepan over medium heat. Gradually stir in polenta. Reduce heat and cook 5 minutes, stirring constantly.   Cover and transfer to oven. Bake until thick but still creamy, add more water if mixture appears too dry, stirring occasionally, about 45 minutes. Remove from oven. Stir in creme fraiche, grated cheeses, and butter. Spoon polenta onto plates and top with roasted mushrooms.

Mushrooms: Preheat oven to 425° degrees. Line two baking sheets with foil. Combine garlic, olive oil, vinegar, rosemary, and thyme in bowl. Add mushrooms and toss to coat. Arrange in single layer on prepared baking sheets. Roast until mushrooms are tender and slightly crisp on edges, about 25 minutes.

Pate and Port Aspic

Chicken Pate
3/4 pound chicken livers
1 cup whole milk
1/2 cup port
1 cup butter, room
    temperature
3/4 cup sliced onion
1/2 tart green apple,
    peeled, cored
    and sliced
3 tablespoons heavy
    cream
1 teaspoon salt, to taste
1 teaspoon lemon juice

Rinse livers and drain. Combine milk and 1/4 cup port. Add livers to mixture and soak for 1 hour. Melt 1/2 cup butter over medium heat. Saute onion until translucent, add apple slices and saute until softened. Cool mixture and transfer to blender.

Saute drained livers over medium high heat until cooked, about 10 minutes. Cool and transfer to blender.

Reduce heat to medium, add 1/4 cup port to skillet and cook, scraping the browned bits clinging to the bottom. Reduce slightly. Add cream to skillet to warm and pour into blender. Puree mixture in blender with start-and-stop motions, scraping down sides until mixture is smooth in consistency. Let stand until lukewarm. Cream remaining butter and gradually add to blender while it is running, blending well. Mix in salt and lemon juice. Pour over chilled aspic and refrigerate several hours until set. To serve, set mold in warm water briefly. Run sharp knife around edge of pate and invert onto serving tray. Decorate with mounds of parsley and colorful flowers for an elegant presentation. Surround with sliced baguette or water crackers.

(Continued on next page)

Port Aspic

2 teaspoons unflavored
  gelatin
1 cup port wine
1 tablespoon sugar
1 tablespoon water
3 tablespoons red
  wine vinegar
1 tablespoon fresh
  tarragon, chopped fine
  or 1/2 teaspoon dried

Generously butter loaf pan. Dissolve gelatin in small bowl with 1/4 cup port. In medium saucepan, combine sugar and water and stir until dissolved over medium high heat. Watch the mixture cook, it will foam up and finally turn to a dark, caramel colored syrup, in about 5 to 7 minutes. Remove from heat and whisk in vinegar, remaining port and tarragon. Stir until the carmel dissolves. Return to low heat and simmer 2 minutes. Add gelatin, stirring until dissolved.

Strain aspic through a cheesecloth-lined strainer into prepared pan covering 1/4 to 3/8 inch of bottom. Cover pan in plastic wrap, refrigerate until set. Can be prepared a day in advance.

Thai Meatballs

Thai Cucumber Sauce

2 pickling cucumbers,
    quartered and thinly
    sliced
2 fresh red chilies, seeded
    and chopped
2 large cloves of garlic
1/2 to 1 tablespoon sugar
1/2 of 1 lime, juiced
1/4 cup vinegar
1 to 2 shallots, thinly sliced
1 handful of fresh
    cilantro leaves
2 tablespoons roasted peanuts,
    coarsely chopped

Pound chilies and garlic to a
paste. Combine with remaining ingredients. Serve with
Thai Meatballs.

3/4 pound ground beef
1/4 pound ground pork
1/2 cup minced
    green onion
2 tablespoons chopped
    cilantro
2 tablespoons soy sauce
1 tablespoon minced
    garlic
1/2 teaspoon grated
    nutmeg
1/4 teaspoon salt
1/4 teaspoon pepper
1 egg beaten
1 12-ounce package of
    fresh Chinese noodles
vegetable oil for frying

Blend all ingredients but egg and noodles in large bowl. Can be prepared 1 day ahead and refrigerated. Bring to room temperature before using. Roll mixture into tiny meatballs 1 to 1 1/4 inch in diameter. Dip meatball into egg. Beginning at base, wrap noodle randomly around meatball as if winding a ball of yarn. Add an additional noodle if desired. Repeat with remaining meatballs. Can also be prepared 1 day ahead. Wrap in plastic and refrigerate if delaying cooking.

Heat oil in deep fryer or saucepan to 375°. Add meatballs in batches and fry until golden brown, about 4 to 5 minutes. Drain. Serve hot or at room temperature with sauce.

Sesame Chicken Bites

2 eggs
2 tablespoons sake wine
2 tablespoons grated
   lemon peel
2 tablespoons sugar
2 tablespoons grated fresh
   ginger or 1 tablespoon
   dried ginger
2 teaspoons salt
2 teaspoons minced garlic
2 pounds boned chicken
   breasts cut into 1 x 1
   inch pieces

vegetable oil for frying
3/4 cup minus 2 table-
   spoons corn starch
1/2 cup sesame seeds

Apricot-Mustard Sauce:
1 tablespoon dry mustard
1 teaspoon water
vegetable oil
1 12-ounce jar apricot
   preserves or apricot jelly

Blend first 7 ingredients in a shallow bowl. Add chicken and mix thoroughly. Let stand at room temperature for 30 minutes or refrigerate overnight. Heat oil in deep saucepan to 400° or until bread cube dropped into hot oil fries to golden brown immediately. Stir cornstarch into chicken mixture. Coat each chicken piece with sesame seeds, shaking off excess. Add chicken in batches and fry until golden brown, 2 minutes. Drain on paper towels. Serve hot or at room temperature with mustard dip or sweet and sour sauce.

To prepare apricot-mustard sauce mix mustard with enough water to form paste. Blend in several drops of oil. Process preserves until smooth. Blend mustard with apricot preserves. Add water to thin if necessary.

Trixie's Cannellini Bean Soup

Geano Abraham
Allegro Gourmet Pizzeria

1 pound cannellini beans
5 cups vegetable or
   beef stock
5 cups water
3 to 5 pounds ham
   with bone
1/2 cup unsalted butter
1/2 head celery, diced

1 pound carrots, diced
1 onion, diced
1/2 tablespoon chopped
   garlic
3 tablespoons chopped
   fresh Italian parsley
1/4 teaspoon fresh
   black pepper

Soak beans for 1 hour.

Combine stock and water in a large pot and bring to boil.

Rinse ham to remove salt. Remove meat from bone. Remove fat from meat in large pieces. Add fat and bone to pot. Add beans

In another pan cook vegetables lightly in butter. Add to soup pot. Add pepper.

Cut ham into 1/2 inch cubes. Remove all fat. Add ham cubes to soup pot and cook until all vegetables are tender, beans are cooked and broth is thick. Remove bone and fat. Skim oil from top. Serve with sourdough French bread.

This recipe makes about 5 quarts and freezes well.

19th Hole Tomato Consomme

4 cups chicken stock
16-ounce can chopped
    tomatoes with juice
2 teaspoons tomato paste
1/2 teaspoon thyme
1/2 teaspoon basil
1/2 teaspoon allspice
2 teaspoons lemon juice
2 tablespoons dry sherry
2 tablespoons chopped
    parsley

Mix all ingredients except sherry and parsley in saucepan. Simmer for 15 minutes. Add sherry and garnish with parsley.

Serves six.

"If I had only one round of golf to play, I would play it at Pebble Beach,"– Jack Nicklaus

It's understandable why Jack Nicklaus feels that way. He won the 1961 U.S. Amateur and the 1972 U.S. Open at Pebble Beach Golf Links, the only man to win those two tournaments on the same course. He only narrowly lost the 1982 U.S. Open held there to Tom Watson.

Crowning his achievements at Pebble Beach are three Bing Crosby National Pro-Am Titles - 1967, 1972 and 1973.

Red and Yellow Roasted Pepper Soup

Wendy Brodie
Rancho San Carlos

This recipe requires two separate batches of soup, one red and one yellow. Use 8 red peppers in one batch and 8 yellow peppers in the other. The ingredients for each batch of soup are as follows:

8 bell peppers
2 tablespoons peanut oil or oil of choice
1 large yellow onion, chopped
2 large shallots, chopped
2 cloves garlic, chopped
3/4 cup dry sherry
1 quart chicken stock
sachet: 1 bay leaf, 1 tablespoon black peppercorns, 3 sprigs fresh thyme, 1 sprig fresh basil, 1 large sprig fresh parsley, tied in cheesecloth

Cilantro Pesto

4 bunches or cups of cilantro
4 cloves garlic
1/4 cup Asiago or hard Parmesan cheese, grated
1/2 cup pumpkin seeds
1/2 lime, juiced
1 serrano chili, roasted, peeled, seeded
1 1/2 cups olive oil
salt and pepper to taste

Mix together in blender until smooth.

Roast bell peppers until skin turns black. Place peppers in a plastic bag and secure end. Allow peppers to steam in bag for about 10 minutes to loosen skin. Remove from bag and pull off skin and take seeds out. Chop in large pieces and set aside. Heat oil in large saucepan over medium heat and saute onion, shallots, and garlic. Add sherry and cook for about 15 minutes or until liquid evaporates. Add chicken stock and sachet. Cook for about another 10 minutes. Add peppers and simmer a little longer. Remove sachet. Place soup in blender and blend until smooth. Cool. Repeat for the second batch of soup.

When serving place a form such as cardboard wrapped with plastic wrap in the middle of each soup bowl. Pour one batch of each colored soup on either side of form. Remove form and top with creme fraiche, cilantro pesto, and fried tortilla strips.

Serves eight to ten.

Orange Carrot Soup

3 tablespoons butter
1 onion, sliced thinly
1 pound carrots, peeled
    and sliced
1 quart chicken stock
1 cup fresh orange juice
1/2 can orange juice
    concentrate

Melt butter in sauce pan. Saute onions in butter until translucent. Add carrots and continue cooking until limp. Puree onion and carrot mixture. In stock pot heat chicken stock and add carrot and onion puree. Cool. Stir in orange juice and concentrate. May be seasoned with fresh ginger.

Serves eight.

If you want to build the greatest golf course in the world, hire an amateur. That's what Samuel F.B. Morse did.

When Morse hired Jack Neville, two-time California State Amateur Champion and a member of the winning 1923 U.S. Walker Cup Team, to lay out the world's most famous golf course, Neville was a real estate salesman for Del Monte Properties and had never designed a golf course.

Morse had decided that the golf course, not homes, would border the ocean. Neville then walked the land for three weeks, deciding to place as many holes along the water as possible. Very little clearing was necessary; he took advantage of the natural hazards - the beaches, the cliffs, the ocean.

Chilled Pea Soup with Mint

The basic original figure-eight layout of Pebble Beach Golf Links has been unchanged since 1919. The flow of the course, the beauty of the scenery and the natural disasters awaiting a miss-hit ball beckon to golfers all around the world.

The course designer, Jack Neville's, two favorite holes were the par-four eighth and the par-five 18th.

"On the eighth," he once said, "you have to play your second shot directly over a cliff and it must carry 180 yards or it's in the ocean. You can go around the cliff, but it costs you an extra shot.

"On the 18th, the worst thing you can do is hook, because its ocean all down the left side. The fairway gets narrower as you approach the green. The opening on the front side is only about five feet, with sand traps right in front. The small opening makes it difficult to get there in two. I was able to get pin high a couple of times, but I've never been on the green in two."

2 cups fresh peas, shelled
   or frozen peas
1 small onion, sliced
1 cup water with salt
   and pepper
3 cups chicken stock
2 tablespoons
   melted butter
2 tablespoons flour
1/2 cup heavy cream
3 tablespoons fresh
   mint, chopped

Boil the peas and onions in 1 cup water seasoned with salt and pepper, until very tender, 7 to 10 minutes. Melt butter and flour together until bubbly, but not browned. Add the chicken stock and heat over medium heat stirring constantly, until mixture is thickened. Press peas though a strainer and add to the stock, or puree all in a blender to get a smooth texture. Bring to a boil. Add heavy cream and chill. Taste for seasoning after chilling soup as flavors become more subdued when cold. Just before serving sprinkle with finely chopped mint.

Serves six.

Fall Greens Soup

2 tablespoons butter
2 yellow onions, chopped
4 medium zucchini,
    chopped
4 cups chicken stock
l bunch fresh spinach,
    stems removed
12 large fresh basil leaves
    or 1 1/2 teaspoons
    dried basil
l tablespoon lemon juice
salt and pepper to taste

Melt butter in soup pot. Add onions, cook covered 20 minutes, over low heat until soft but not browned. Add zucchini and cook covered 5 minutes. Add stock, bring to boil, reduce heat and cook covered for 20 minutes. Remove from heat. Stir in spinach and basil. Cover, and let rest 5 minutes. Cool. Puree in blender. Return to soup pot. Season with salt and pepper. Stir in lemon juice.

Serves four.

It is a very rich soup, tastes creamy, but is low in calories.

*P*ebble Beach has been hosting golf tournaments since 1919 when it was first built for the California State Men's Amateur tournament. Pebble Beach Golf Links has made its name through hosting tournaments of national and international significance ever since.

Three United States Open championships have been hosted at The Pebble Beach Golf Links in 1972, 1982 and 1992. Pebble Beach will again be host to the U. S. Open in 2000.

Asparagus Soup Crutee

1 quart milk
3 cups chicken stock
1 cup cold water
7 tablespoons butter
6 tablespoons flour
2 pounds thin asparagus
    spears, bottom of
    stalks trimmed
8 slices French bread
3/4 cup grated
    Parmesan cheese
white pepper
fresh nutmeg

In a large saucepan, combine milk, stock and, water. Heat to boiling. Set aside. In a 4 quart soup kettle, melt half the butter. Add flour and stir over low heat until flour is cooked and blond. Remove from heat. Whisk in hot milk mixture, add asparagus. Cover and heat to simmering. Set cover ajar and simmer until spears are very soft, about 40 minutes.

Meanwhile, place bread slices on baking sheet. Brush with remaining butter and bake at 400° until lightly browned, turning once, set aside.

In 2 cups batches, puree cooked asparagus mixture. Return pureed soup to kettle. Stir in cream and season to taste. Top each bread slice with 2 tablespoons cheese and melt under a broiler. Serve soup with the crouton on top. If desired, add cream for thicker and richer soup.

Serves eight.

Artichoke Soup

8 to 10 large artichokes
1 gallon of water with
    6 lemons squeezed
    into it
1/4 cup olive oil
2 yellow onions, sliced
8 cloves garlic, coarsely
    chopped
3 tomatoes, halved
2 quarts chicken stock
1/4 bunch fresh thyme
1 1/2 cups cream
salt, pepper and hot
    sauce to taste

Trim tops and tough part of stem from artichokes. Peel tough outer leaves from artichokes and discard. Peel leaves until artichokes are almost down to the hearts; remove chokes. Cut artichokes into quarters and reserve in lemon water, to help from discoloring. In large stock pot, saute onions in olive oil until beginning to brown. Drain artichokes. Add all ingredients in pot except for cream. Simmer for 1 1/2 hours until artichokes are soft. Pass soup through large holes of food mill, or puree in blender in batches, stirring to combine. Return soup to a boil in a saucepan. Add cream and season with salt, pepper and Tabasco.

Serves ten.

Im Ladris Onion Soup

*T*he stock is best if home made. Make it the day before from any standard beef stock recipe. It can be made weeks before and frozen. If freezing stock, reduce greatly, pour into ice cube trays to freeze. Reconstitute by adding water. If canned broth is used, eliminate the salt and add a couple of bouillon cubes to give added taste.

❧

12 cups thinly sliced
   yellow onions
2 tablespoons butter
2 tablespoons
   vegetable oil
1/2 teaspoon sugar
3 tablespoons flour

2 quarts beef stock
3/4 cup dry white wine
1/4 cup brandy
French bread baguette
1 cup Parmesan or Swiss
   cheese, grated

In a large covered saucepan, cook the onions over low heat in the butter and oil, stirring occasionally. After the onions have wilted raise the heat to moderate and add the salt and sugar. Stirring frequently cook the onions until they are a dark brown, almost caramelized. This can take 1 to 1 1/2 hours. Scrape the bottom of the pan often with a wooden spoon and be careful to regulate the heat so they do not burn. When the onions are deeply colored add the flour and stir for 3 to 4 minutes to cook the flour.

In a separate saucepan bring the broth to a boil, add the wine and then add the liquids to the onions. Partially cover and simmer at low heat for 1 hour. Just before serving add brandy.

To serve, place rounds of toasted French bread in soup cups and pour the soup over them and top with grated Parmesan or Swiss cheese. Preheat oven to 450°. Place onion soup in individual oven proof soup pots. Float rounds of French bread on top and spread the cheese over them. Cook for 5 minutes or until the cheese melts.

Serves eight to ten.

❧

Sweet Potato, Corn & Jalapeno Soup

1/4 cup unsalted butter
1 small onion,
    finely chopped
1 1/2 pounds sweet
    potatoes, peeled
    and chopped
6 cups chicken stock
1 1/2 cups fresh corn
    kernels, may
    use frozen corn
2 teaspoons finely
    chopped jalapeno
    pepper, seeds removed
1/2 cup heavy cream

Melt butter in large saucepan over medium heat. Add onion and saute until tender, about 6 minutes. Add sweet potatoes and stock and bring to a boil. Reduce heat and simmer until potatoes are tender, about 30 minutes. Strain, using coarse sieve to separate stock mixture from sweet potatoes. Return stock mixture to saucepan. Transfer sweet potatoes from sieve to processor and puree. Whisk puree into stock mixture. Add corn and jalapeno peppers and simmer 5 minutes. Add cream to soup and stir until heated through.

Serves four to six.

Point Joe's Clam Soup

1 teaspoon chopped
  garlic
2 tablespoons olive oil
2 pounds ripe tomatoes,
  peeled, seeded, and
  finely chopped (or use
  3 cups drained and
  chopped canned
  Italian plum tomatoes)
2 cups dry white wine

1 cup water
2 dozen small hard shell
  clams, thoroughly
  washed and scrubbed
2 tablespoons chopped
  fresh parsley,
  preferably Italian
cheesecloth for
  straining broth

In a 2 to 3 quart saucepan, saute garlic briefly in hot olive oil. Stir in wine and tomatoes and bring to a boil. Reduce heat to low, partially cover pan, and simmer for 10 minutes, stirring occasionally. Meanwhile, in 10 to 12 inch skillet pour in 1/3-inch layer of water. Bring to high boil and drop in clams, covering pan tightly. Steam clams over high heat for 5 to 10 minutes, until they open. Discard any that remain persistently closed. Transfer the clams, still in their shells, to 4 heated soup plates. Strain the remaining clam broth through a fine sieve, lined with cheesecloth to remove any sand, into the simmering tomato sauce. Boil for 1 to 2 minutes, taste for seasoning, and pour mixture over the clams. Sprinkle the top with parsley and serve immediately with plenty of hot French or Italian bread.

Serves four.

Clambake Chowder

1 medium onion
1 stalk celery
1/2 cup butter
1/2 teaspoon white
    pepper
1 bay leaf
1 clove minced garlic
1/4 teaspoon thyme
1/2 teaspoon salt
1/2 cup flour
40 ounces clam juice
1 large potato, peeled
    and chopped
1 pint heavy cream
1 large can of clams,
    minced or whole

Drain clams and reserve liquid. Rinse clams in water and drain again. In large pot, combine butter, and garlic. Saute 2-3 minutes. Add onions, celery and spices. Saute until onions are translucent. Add flour and stir constantly. Cook over low heat for 5 minutes, do not brown. Slowly add clam juice stirring constantly to avoid lumps. Simmer for 10 minutes. The soup will be very thick at this point, be careful not to burn. Add potatoes and cook until tender. Add cream and clams and bring to a boil.

Serves four to six.

Pebble Beach is famous as the home of the Bing Crosby National Pro-Am, now the AT&T Pebble Beach National Pro-Am.

Known as "The Clambake" for the party preceding play, crooner Bing Crosby brought the tournament to Pebble Beach in 1947. To attract an audience, Crosby matched celebrities with professionals for the entire tournament, expanded play to three courses, and gave the proceeds to local charities.

The weather was often horrendous - in 1962 the fourth round was postponed due to an overnight snowfall - but the beauty of Pebble Beach mixed with great golf from the professionals and antics from the celebrities was tailor made for television audiences. Crosby played until 1957 and the following year became the tournament's television analyst.

After Crosby's death, the tournament was kept alive by his sons, and then received corporate sponsorship from the AT&T Company in 1986.

Oysters Rockefeller Soup

1 package of frozen
   leaf spinach
2 shallots or 2 green
   onions, tops and all
2 inner stalks of celery,
   chopped, leaves and all
1 1/2 cups chicken broth
2 cups whole milk or
   half and half
1/4 teaspoon anise
   seed, ground
2 dashes hot sauce
1/4 teaspoon salt
1 tablespoon thyme
2 12-ounce jars
   of oysters

In a large pot add spinach, shallots and celery to the chicken broth and bring to a boil. Boil until all ingredients are tender, about 10 minutes. Remove from heat and puree. Return pureed mixture to pot. Add the milk or half and half, the seasoning and the oysters. Bring to a gentle boil and cook until oysters are tender.

Serves six.

SALADS & VEGETABLES

Salinas

I t is the salad bowl of the nation. Ninety percent of the nation's green, leafy vegetables are grown in the fertile Salinas Valley, embellished by the tomatoes, broccoli, and other row crops that line the fields. The home of rancheros, the city now ranks among the major agri-business centers in the world.

Nestled between the Santa Lucia mountains and the Gabilan range the culture of Salinas grows from the rich loam of the surrounding soil. The people take their strength from the earth, their inspiration from their heritage, and their vegetables straight from the fields.

Spinach Salad with Chutney Mustard Dressing

1 bunch fresh spinach,
  stemmed
4-5 pieces bacon,
  fried crisp, drained
  and crumbled
2 hard-boiled eggs,
  shelled and sliced
5 mushrooms, sliced
1 ripe avocado, chopped
1/2 cup diced red onions

Chutney Mustard Dressing
2 teaspoons sugar
1/4 cup white
  wine vinegar
1 garlic clove, minced
3 tablespoons chutney
2 teaspoons dry mustard
1/3 - 1/2 cup olive oil

Wash the spinach well, discard stems and tear into small pieces. Add the bacon, eggs, mushrooms, avocado and onions. Toss with the dressing.

Dressing: Combine all ingredients except oil in blender or food processor. With motor running, add the oil in a thin stream and combine until smooth.

Serves four.

Wedding Spinach Salad with Yogurt Dressing

1/2 pound spinach, stems
  removed, torn up
1/2 small cucumber,
  thinly sliced
2 fresh peaches, sliced
3 fresh plums, sliced
1/8 cup green onion,
  sliced

Yogurt Dressing
1 cup lemon
  low fat yogurt
1 tablespoon fresh
  lemon juice
1 tablespoon water
1/3 teaspoon dried
  dill weed or
  1 teaspoon chopped
  fresh dill weed

Wash and drain spinach. Combine with the rest of the salad ingredients. Blend yogurt dressing ingredients together and add to spinach mixture.

Serves four to six.

Pacific Rim Spinach Salad

1 large bunch spinach,
   stemmed, washed
   thoroughly, patted
   dry and torn into
   large pieces
1 8-ounce can sliced
   water chestnuts,
   drained
1 cup fresh bean sprouts
1/2 cup cooked,
   chopped bacon
2 hard-boiled eggs, grated

Dressing
1 medium onion,
   finely chopped
1 cup safflower oil
1/2 cup sugar
1/3 cup catsup
1/3 cup red wine vinegar

Combine spinach with water chestnuts in a large serving bowl. Thoroughly mix all dressing ingredients and toss with spinach and water chestnuts. Layer bean sprouts over the dressed spinach. Then sprinkle bacon pieces and finally top with grated egg.

Serves four.

The name Salinas comes from the Spanish word "salina" or salty. The town is named for the salt marshes that lie between the Salinas River and the sand dunes of the Pacific Ocean. In Spanish California, the production of salt was a royal monopoly and one of the governor's responsibilities was to guard the salt marshes until the salt was hard and ready to dry. Spanish cavalry then bagged the salt and brought it to Monterey for sale.

Greek Spinach Salad

2 bunches spinach,
washed, stemmed and
torn into pieces
1/4 pound Feta cheese,
crumbled
3 tablespoons minced
red onion
3/4 cup cooked
black beans
1/4 cup Greek olives,
pitted
1/2 cup croutons

Dressing
1/2 cup olive oil
3 tablespoons red
wine vinegar
3 tablespoons lemon juice
1 1/2 teaspoons tarragon
1 clove garlic, minced
salt & pepper to taste

Mix the spinach, 1/2 the Feta cheese, onion, 1/2 the black beans, olives and croutons together.

Whisk the salad dressing together. Pour over salad and toss well. Add the remaining cheese and beans for a garnish to the salad.

Serves six to eight.

Sicilian Salad

1 head butter lettuce
4 ripe roma tomatoes,
   diced
1/2 cup fresh basil leaves,
   chopped
1 1/2 cups cubed Buffalo
   Mozzarella cheese
1/4 cup basalmic vinegar
1/2 cup olive oil
2 cloves garlic, minced
salt and pepper to taste

Tear lettuce into pieces. Combine with tomatoes, basil and cheese. Whisk vinegar, oil, garlic, salt and pepper together. Toss over salad.

Serves four.

If it is in your salad, chances are it is from Salinas. Often referred to as the "Salad Bowl for the World", eighty percent of America's commercially grown lettuce, ninety percent of its broccoli, fifty percent of its mushrooms and cauliflower, twenty-five percent of its celery and one hundred percent of the nation's artichokes are grown in Monterey County.

Caesar Salad with a Heart

1/2 cup grated Parmesan
   cheese
1 head romaine lettuce,
   washed, dried and torn
   into pieces
2 6 1/2 ounce jars
   marinated artichokes,
   reserving juice
   from both jars
1 cup croutons

Dressing
2 egg yolks
oil from artichokes
1/3 cup olive oil
2 teaspoons fresh
   lemon juice
2 teaspoons Dijon
   mustard
2-3 cloves garlic, pressed
   or finely minced

Use all or a combination of:
1 bunch green onions,
   chopped
6 mint leaves, chopped
2 tomatoes, peeled
   and chopped
1/2 pound bacon,
   browned and crumbled

Assemble salad, using lettuce, artichokes, onions, mint, tomatoes and bacon. Blend dressing ingredients. Toss over salad. Add grated Parmesan cheese and croutons and toss again.

Serves four to six.

Leeks Vinaigrette

1 bunch leeks
2 hard-boiled eggs,
    chopped
2 medium shallots, finely
    chopped
1 tablespoon chopped
    parsley

Vinaigrette dressing
2 tablespoons white
    wine vinegar
6 tablespoons oil
salt and pepper to taste

Trim the leeks, removing the outer leaves. Split them lengthwise, almost to the root and wash thoroughly. Tie in bundles and cook in boiling, salted water for 8-12 minutes or until tender. Drain, refresh with cold water. Drain again. Squeeze to remove excess liquid. Remove string. Cut leeks in 1/3's and arrange on platter. Add chopped egg, parsley and shallots. Whisk vinaigrette together. Spoon dressing over leeks. Serve at room temperature.

This recipe can also be prepared using asparagus. If so, do not refresh with cold water. Serve warm. Spoon dressing over center of asparagus, leaving heads and ends uncoated.

Serves four.

Summary Pear Salad

Lettuce, the major cash crop of the Salinas Valley, did not make its agricultural debut until 1921. In that year, a few plots of land along the Salinas River were planted in lettuce, producing a surprising bumper crop. The heads were huge and the crop yielded 400 crates per acre. Sixty-eight freight cars carried the first year's harvest to the East Coast markets.

Within 10 years that amount had increased to 20,000 cars a year. In the years before refrigeration, when produce was carried in iced railroad cars, the difference between agricultural success and financial ruin lay in the ability to get the lettuce crop across the country without the summer heat ruining the heads.

1 head butter lettuce, rinsed, drained and torn
2 bosc pears, halved and peeled
1/2 cup whole walnuts, toasted in a skillet until lightly browned
3 ounces blue cheese, crumbled

Dressing
1/2 cup extra light olive oil
1/4 cup red wine vinegar
1 teaspoon honey mustard
2 tablespoons balsamic vinegar
1/2 teaspoon salt
1/2 teaspoon fresh ground pepper
1 tablespoon honey

Divide lettuce equally on four plates. Take half of a pear and slice lengthwise to make a fan on top of lettuce. Sprinkle with walnuts and crumbled blue cheese. Mix dressing well and drizzle over assembled salad.

It's elegant and, above all, quick to make.

Serves four.

Avocado and Cantaloupe with Tangy Citrus Dressing

1 cantaloupe, seeded,
   peeled and cut into
   1 inch pieces
2 medium avocados,
   peeled and cut into
   1/4 inch thick slices
1 14-ounce can of
   hearts of palm, diced
2 tablespoons lemon juice
1/2 cup slivered
   almonds, toasted
2 tablespoons butter,
   melted
1 head butter lettuce

Tangy Citrus Dressing
6 tablespoons lemon juice
6 tablespoons lime juice
1/2 teaspoon white
   pepper
1/2 teaspoon
   ground ginger

Combine cantaloupes, avocados and hearts of palm in a large bowl. Sprinkle with lemon juice and refrigerate covered for one hour. Place dressing ingredients in a jar with a tight lid and shake. To toast almonds drizzle with 2 tablespoons melted butter and bake at 325° for 15 minutes. Tear butter lettuce into large bite-sized pieces and line serving bowl. Spoon fruit mixture into center. Pour dressing over salad and sprinkle with almonds.

Serves six to eight.

Festive Greens and Citrus Salad with Hazelnut Vinaigrette

2 Belgian endive, sliced
   into 1/4 inch rounds
2 bunches watercress,
   long stems removed
1 fennel bulb, sliced
   very thin
1 blood orange, peeled
   and sectioned
1/4 cup hazelnuts, toasted
   and coarsely chopped

Vinaigrette
2 tablespoons white
   wine vinegar
2 tablespoons hazelnut oil
1/3 cup olive oil
1/2 cup blood orange
   juice, from
   about 1-2 oranges
pinch of salt and pepper
1 teaspoon finely
   chopped shallots

For vinaigrette, mix ingredients thoroughly with a wire whisk in small mixing bowl.

Toss endive, watercress and fennel with the vinaigrette. Decorate with the blood orange sections and sprinkle with chopped hazelnuts.

Serves four.

Watercress and Orange Salad

1 head of lettuce, washed,
    drained and torn
2 bunches watercress,
    washed with large
    stems removed
4 large oranges

Lemon Dressing
6 tablespoons lemon juice
6 tablespoons olive oil
1 clove garlic, pressed
2 teaspoons sugar
1/2 teaspoon salt
1/2 teaspoon freshly
    ground black pepper

Line the salad bowl with the lettuce in bite-sized pieces. Place the watercress in a layer on top of the lettuce. To make the orange slices, peel the oranges and cut off the white membrane with a sharp knife. Slice crosswise into thin slices. Cover with orange slices. Whisk all lemon dressing ingredients together. Pour Lemon Dressing over salad just before serving.

Great with turkey or beef for Thanksgiving or Christmas.

Serves six to eight.

How do you improve a strawberry? Ask the folks at Driscoll Strawberry Associates, the country's largest producer of fresh strawberries.

When the strawberry industry began in the Salinas Valley in the early 1900s, most strawberry plants produced a single crop per growing season. University of California researchers began developing "everbearing" varieties of berries to take advantage of the area's temperate climate and year round sunshine.

Over the past 50 years, Driscoll has continued development of strawberries, leading to many patented strains.

Driscoll strawberries have long been sought by restauranteurs and are now available at supermarkets in special environmentally friendly packages bearing the Driscoll name.

Pastures of Heaven Salad

1 bunch fresh spinach,
   washed, dried
   and stemmed
2 oranges, peeled
   and diced
1 head Romaine lettuce
   or Bibb lettuce
1/2 cup sliced almonds
fresh raspberries for
   garnish, optional

Dressing
1/2 cup vegetable oil
3 tablespoons raspberry
   vinegar
1 tablespoons sugar
1 clove garlic, peeled
   and crushed
1/3 cup fresh orange juice
salt and pepper to taste

Toss spinach, oranges, lettuce and almonds together. Whisk the dressing ingredients. Pour over salad. Garnish with fresh raspberries.

Serves six to eight.

California Garden Salad with Sweet Vinaigrette

1 head Romaine lettuce
1 11-ounce can mandarin
   oranges, chilled
1 cup sliced almonds,
   toasted

Dressing
1/2 cup sugar
1/2 teaspoon
   seasoned salt
1/2 teaspoon dry mustard
3 tablespoons wine
   vinegar
1 cup vegetable oil
1/4 cup dry white wine
1/4 cup minced onion,
   preferably red

Wash and tear lettuce into bite-sized pieces. Drain oranges and toss with lettuce and almonds. Place all dressing ingredients in blender and blend until well mixed and onion is finely minced. Chill and serve over salad.

Serves four to six.

Salinas secured its place in the Guiness Book of Records as the nation's salad bowl in 1988 when Salinas Valley Fair officials tossed the World's Largest Salad. Over 36,000 heads of lettuce were used.

Wing Chong Chinese Salad Dressing

2 tablespoons soy sauce
2 tablespoons sesame
    seed oil
2 tablespoons rice
    wine vinegar
1/4 cup salad oil
1/2 teaspoon dry mustard
2 tablespoons sugar
1 teaspoon finely
    chopped or grated
    fresh ginger
2-3 tablespoons of
    chopped fresh cilantro
    to taste

Mix all ingredients in a blender at high speed. Add the cilantro last, pulsing just to combine. This is good on any chicken salad combination with chow mein noodles or fried rice sticks, with pickled ginger, etc. It is also excellent on a mixed green salad with grilled shrimp.

Makes 3/4 cup of dressing.

Garlic Mint Salad Dressing

1 large garlic clove,
    crushed
2 tablespoons fresh
    lime juice
1 1/2-2 teaspoons
    chopped fresh
    mint leaves
pinch of sugar
1/4 teaspoon salt
1/3 cup vegetable oil

In a blender or food processor, blend garlic, mustard, mint, sugar and salt, scraping down the sides until mixture is smooth. With motor running, add oil in a stream and blend until emulsified.

Makes 1/2 cup of dressing.

Spreckels Poppy Seed Dressing

Sugar beets were the first crop that turned the deep brown earth into gold for the Salinas farmers. The financial return from sugar beets was assured when Claus Spreckles built a sugar refinery near Salinas, and contracted with local farmers for 25,000 acres of sugar beets annually. For the farmer, there was no risk - the Spreckels plant would buy everything he grew.

1/4 cup sugar
1 teaspoon dry mustard
salt to taste
1/3 cup white wine
    vinegar
2 shallots, finely minced
1 cup salad oil
1 1/2 teaspoons poppy
    seeds

In blender, add sugar, mustard, salt, vinegar and shallots. Blend thoroughly. Add oil and blend on high speed. Stir in poppy seeds. Taste for seasoning. Refrigerate before serving.

A wonderful dressing on any salad with fruit in it.

Makes 1 1/2 cups of dressing.

Rancho San Lucas Dressing

dash of cayenne
1/2 teaspoon dry mustard
1 teaspoon
    worchestershire sauce
1 tablespoon finely
    minced onion
1 clove garlic, minced
2 tablespoons garlic
    vinegar
6 tablespoons salad oil
salt and pepper to taste

Whisk all ingredients together.

Makes 1/2 cup salad dressing.

Gingered Cucumber Salad

12 ounces snow peas,
   strings removed
4 pounds English hot-
   house cucumbers
   Halve lengthwise.
   Scoop out seeds, peel
   and cut into 1/4 inch
   slices.
2 8-ounce cans water
   chestnuts, drained
1 cup chopped
   green onion
2 heaping tablespoons
   minced fresh ginger

Dressing
1/2 cup oil
1/4 cup rice vinegar
1/2 teaspoon white pepper
salt to taste

Blanch snow peas in boiling, salted water for one minute. Drain, refresh in cold water and pat dry. Combine snow peas, cucumbers, chestnuts, onion and ginger. Whisk together oil, rice vinegar, pepper and salt. Mix salad and dressing together and serve on lettuce leaf.

Great with salmon.

Serves eight.

Laureles Caponata

Jon Kasky
Bird of Paradise Catering

1 large eggplant, diced,
    skin on
2 tablespoons olive oil
1 onion, diced
1 cup tomatoes, peeled,
    seeded and diced
1/2 cup black pitted
    olives, sliced

1/2 cup green pitted
    olives, sliced
1 tablespoon capers
2 tablespoons blond
    raisins
1 tablespoon vinegar
1/4 cup dry red wine
1/4 cup toasted pine nuts

In a large skillet, quickly brown the diced eggplant in the olive oil over high heat. Remove the eggplant to a saucepan. Add the onions and cook until they become translucent. Add the remaining ingredients, except the pinenuts, and simmer one hour until nearly dry. Taste and season with salt and pepper. Add pinenuts just before serving. Serve hot or cold. Keeps and improves over one week.

Serve on a lettuce leaf with croutons on the side.

Makes about two cups.

Steinbeck Country Salad

1 1/2 cups mushrooms, sliced

1 1/2 cups cherry tomatoes, cut in half

1 1/2 cups zucchini, sliced

1 1/2 cups carrots, thinly sliced

1 1/2 cups scallions, chopped

1 1/2 cups broccoli, broken into florets

1 1/2 cups cauliflower, broken into florets

Mix together:

2 cloves garlic, pressed or finely minced

1 teaspoon dry mustard

1 tablespoon minced chives

1/4 cup red wine vinegar

2 tablespoons lemon juice

1 cup extra virgin olive oil

salt and black pepper to taste

Blanch the broccoli, cauliflower and carrots in boiling water for 1 1/2 to 2 minutes. Blanch the zucchini for 30 seconds. Drain the vegetables and refresh in cold water. Pat dry. Pour marinade over vegetables and store in refrigerator 24 hours.

Delicious use of fresh vegetables, and a change from the usual green salad.

Serves eight.

Eden Valley Vegetable Pasta Salad

2 cups halved cherry
  tomatoes or
  chopped tomatoes
3/4 cup peeled and seeded
  cucumber, chopped
3/4 cup halved, sliced
  zucchini
1 small green pepper,
  julienned
2 tablespoons
  chopped onion
1/4 cup red wine vinegar
2 tablespoons salad oil

2 tablespoons sugar
1 tablespoon lemon juice
1 teaspoon fresh basil
  or 1/4 teaspoon
  dried basil, crushed
1 small clove garlic,
  minced
salt and pepper to taste
8 ounces angel hair pasta,
  broken
1 tablespoon salad oil
lettuce leaves

Combine tomatoes, cucumber, zucchini, green pepper and onion in large mixing bowl. Blend vinegar, oil, sugar, lemon juice, parsley, basil, salt and pepper. Pour over vegetable mixture. Cover and chill 2-24 hours. Cook the pasta. Drain and rinse under cold water. Toss with 1 tablespoon oil. Cover and chill.

To serve, put pasta in a lettuce lined bowl. Add the vegetables just before serving and toss.

This is great because it can be done ahead.

Serves eight to ten.

San Benito Mushroom Salad

1 pound fresh
    mushrooms
4 1/2 tablespoons Dijon
    mustard
4 1/2 tablespoons red
    wine vinegar
1/2 teaspoon dried
    tarragon
1/2 teaspoon salt
1/2 teaspoon dried
    oregano

1/4 teaspoon freshly
    ground pepper
3/4 cup olive oil
1 head butter lettuce,
    separated into leaves
1 avocado, peeled, pitted
    and thinly sliced
1/2 cup black olives
3 tablespoons chopped
    parsley

Evenly slice the mushrooms and place them in a bowl.

Combine mustard and vinegar, then add tarragon, salt, oregano and pepper. Add olive oil and blend thoroughly with a whisk. Pour dressing over mushrooms and make sure each slice is coated with dressing. Let stand at room temperature for 2 to 3 hours. Serve on a bed of butter lettuce and garnish with avocado slices, black olives and parsley.

Serves six to eight.

Vegetable Salad with Hazelnut Dressing

1 1/2 pounds sugar
    snap or snow peas,
    stemmed, strings
    removed
1 1/2 pounds green beans,
    cut into 1 inch pieces
2 large broccoli bunches,
    cut into florets

Dressing
1 1/2 cups olive oil
2/3 cup red wine vinegar
2/3 cup orange juice
2 tablespoons grated
    orange peel
3/4 cup hazelnuts,
    toasted, finely chopped
zest of 1 orange, cut into
    thin strips, boiled in
    water for 1 minute to
    remove bitterness

Separately blanch vegetables in boiling water until bright green. Drain and rinse in cold water to stop cooking and preserve color. Combine all vegetables in large bowl. Chill quickly. Whisk dressing ingredients together, then mix in hazelnuts. Pour dressing over vegetables. Garnish with orange zest strips.

Great for spring buffet picnic.

Serves twenty.

The fertile valley, naturally arid, is totally dependent on irrigation for prosperity. After the April rains cease, with no prospect of water from the heavens until winter, farmers begin transporting long pipes across the fields to carry water from the Salinas River to the fields. The river is literally mined for its water. Through the course of the growing season, more water is pumped onto the fields of Salinas than ever reaches the ocean.

Greenfield Broccoli Salad

1 bunch broccoli, cut
    into florets
5 slices bacon, cooked
    crisp and chopped
    into small pieces
1/3 cup raisins
1/4 cup chopped onions
1/2 cup mayonnaise
1/4 cup sugar
1 tablespoon vinegar

Blanch broccoli in boiling water for 1 1/2-2 minutes. Refresh in cold water to stop cooking and pat dry.

Combine all ingredients in medium size bowl. Stir until all ingredients are blended. Chill and serve.

Serves six.

Fresh Peppers Salad

1/2 cup olive oil
2 tablespoons minced
  garlic
1/2 yellow onion, minced
2 red bell peppers,
  julienned
2 green bell peppers,
  julienned
1 yellow bell pepper,
  julienned
2 tomatoes, peeled,
  seeded and coarsely
  chopped

1/4 cup fresh oregano
  leaves, or 2 table-
  spoons dried oregano
salt and fresh ground
  pepper to taste
1/2 red onion, paper-thin
  slices for garnish
2 tablespoons minced
  parsley for garnish
1 tablespoon extra virgin
  olive oil, optional

In large skillet over medium heat, heat olive oil until hot but not smoking. Add garlic and onion and saute about 3 minutes. Add peppers, tomatoes, salt and pepper to skillet and mix gently. Scatter oregano leaves across top. Cover and simmer slowly until peppers are soft, 12 to 15 minutes. Taste for seasonings. Transfer to bowl to cool. Serve peppers at room temperature. Garnish with red onion and parsley. If desired, drizzle with extra olive oil.

Serves four.

Vegetables are not the only crops to grow in the fertile Salinas soil. Blossoms fill the fields as eighty percent of the flowers grown for commercial use in the United States sprout from seed in the Salinas Valley.

Blue Cheese and Walnut Potato Salad

2 pounds small red
    potatoes, cut into
    1 inch pieces
1/4 pound, about 1/2 cup,
    blue cheese
1/3 cup mayonnaise
1 1/2 tablespoons fresh
    lemon juice
1 1/2 cup finely chopped
    celery
1/2 cup walnuts,
    chopped coarsely and
    lightly toasted
1/2 cup finely chopped
    dill pickle
1 teaspoon celery seeds

Steam potatoes for 8 to 10 minutes or until just tender. Transfer them to a bowl and let cool. In a blender puree the blue cheese with the mayonnaise, yogurt, lemon juice, salt and pepper. To the potatoes, add the celery, walnuts, pickle, celery seeds and dressing mixture. Toss the salad until it is well combined.

Serves four to six.

Mediterranean Potato Salad

25-30 small red potatoes
4 scallions, sliced
3 cloves garlic, pressed
    or minced
1 cup fresh chopped basil
3/4 cup olive oil
1 small jar capers,
    drained, reserving
    brine
juice of one lemon
1 tablespoon dried basil
salt and pepper to taste

Boil potatoes with skins on for 15-20 minutes or until tender. Drain and quarter. Add sliced scallions, capers and 1/4 cup chopped basil. Combine olive oil, caper brine, lemon juice and dried basil. Shake or stir. Toss potatoes and caper mixture with 3/4 of dressing while potatoes are still warm. Cover. Let sit at room temperature for 1-2 hours. Improves in flavor if made ahead. Just before serving, add the rest of dressing and remaining 3/4 cup fresh basil. Toss gently and serve.

Serves four to six.

Basmati Rice Salad with Arugula and Pine Nuts

*T*he coming of the rail-road meant good times for the Salinas Valley. The rich earth grew all sorts of row crops – beans, corn, tomatoes, celery, lettuce, broccoli – and a cheap, quick, dependable source of transportation to the tables of the East Coast put money in the pockets of farmers. While farming remained a risky business, huge profits were the reward for getting a crop to New York or Boston at the height of the market.

3 cups chicken broth
2 cups basmati rice
5 tablespoons olive oil
3/4 cup slivered
    Kalamata olives
3 tablespoons fresh
    lemon juice
2 ounces fresh arugula,
    chopped
3 green onions, minced
1/2 cup pine nuts, toasted
1/3 cup freshly grated
    Romano cheese
salt and pepper to taste

Cook rice until tender in chicken broth. Fluff with fork. Transfer to large bowl. Mix in olive oil, then remaining ingredients. Season to taste with salt and pepper. Serve at room temperature.

Serves eight.

Glazed Prawn Salad

1 tablespoon butter
1 tablespoon olive oil
2 cloves garlic, minced
1/2 cup green onion,
   chopped
1 pound prawns, peeled
   and deveined
1 tablespoon balsamic
   vinegar
juice of one lemon
1/2 pound mixed baby
   greens

Balsamic Vinaigarette
1 tablespoon balsamic
   vinegar
1/4 cup olive oil
juice of one lemon
1 clove garlic, minced
1/2 teaspoon salt

Saute onions and garlic in butter and olive oil in a skillet over medium high heat until tender, about 1 minute. Add prawns, cook 3 to 4 minutes until pink, add vinegar and lemon. Chill in the cooking juices, vinegar, and lemon for one hour. Serve over bed of baby greens with vinaigrette.

Serves four.

Artichokes Stuffed with Shrimp Salad

During the year, the fields do not lie fallow for a day. The rich earth can be coaxed to produce as many as three crops a year, and as the first crop is being harvested, the second is readied for planting, and the seed for the third is ordered.

4 medium artichokes	1 tablespoon Dijon mustard
1 tablespoon lemon juice	4 chopped green onions
1 large garlic clove, quartered	1/2 teaspoon dill
1 bay leaf	1/4 teaspoon white pepper
1 cup mayonnaise	1/2 teaspoon salt
1/2 cup chopped celery	1 pound cooked bay shrimp
1 tablespoon lemon juice	

Trim the top leaves of the artichoke, by 1/4. Break off small leaves at base. Cut off any remaining thorny tips. Trim stem.

Bring a quart of water to a boil. Add the lemon juice, garlic and a bay leaf. Put in artichokes, cover and cook for 45 minutes or until leaves pull out easily. Remove artichokes and chill.

Mix the mayonnaise, celery, lemon juice, mustard, onions, dill, salt and pepper well. Stir in shrimp. Chill. Open artichokes and evenly distribute salad mixture into each. Serve with lemon wedge.

Serves four.

Artichoke Chicken Salad

1 head iceberg lettuce,
   washed, drained and
   torn in pieces
1 1/2 cups unmarinated
   artichoke hearts,
   chopped
3 cups chopped
   cooked chicken
3/4 cup sliced almonds,
   toasted
1 cup sliced green onions
chow mein noodles for
   garnish, optional

Dressing
1/2 cup lemon juice
1 cup salad oil
4 tablespoons honey
3 tablespoons sugar
2 tablespoons sesame oil
salt and pepper to taste

Toss salad ingredients together, except chow mein
noodles. Whisk dressing ingredients. Mix dressing and
salad. Garnish with chow mein noodles.
Serves eight.

Oriental Chicken Nut Salad

Dressing
1/2 cup plain yogurt
1/3 cup plain
    peanut butter
1/4 cup milk
3 tablespoon white
    wine vinegar
1 tablespoon peanut oil
1 tablespoon soy sauce
1/2 teaspoon garlic,
    minced
1/4 teaspoon cayenne
1/2 teaspoon salt

6 cups lettuce, torn into
    bite-sized pieces
2 cups cooked, diced
    chicken
1 apple, diced
1 cup cabbage, diced
2 tablespoon chopped
    green onion
1/2 cup unsalted peanuts

Combine all dressing ingredients in blender, mixing until smooth. Chill. Mix salad ingredients. Dress just prior to serving.

Perfect as a main course on a warm summer evening. The dressing can be prepared and stored for several days.

Serves four.

Chicken Carmelo Salad

4 chicken breast halves
　　(steamed, boned
　　and chilled)
1 head Romaine lettuce
　　or mixture of
　　various lettuces
2 ounce bag pecan pieces
2 11-ounce cans
　　mandarin orange
　　segments, drained
3 ounces Roquefort
　　cheese, crumbled

Dressing
1/4 cup olive oil
3 tablespoons raspberry
　　wine vinegar
4 tablespoons minced
　　bermuda onion
4 tablespoons Dijon
　　mustard

Blend ingredients for dressing in blender until thick and smooth. Cut cooked, chilled chicken into bite-size pieces. Gently toss chicken, pecans, mandarin oranges and Roquefort with dressing to coat. Present on bed of lettuce. Garnish with nasturtium flowers.

Serves six.

Carrots Madeira

John Steinbeck learned first-hand the difficulties facing America's farm laborers. Born in Salinas February 27, 1902, his father was the county treasurer, his mother a school teacher.

Steinbeck's major works are based on what he knew - life in Salinas and along Cannery Row. He knew the Salinas Valley where *The Red Pony* roamed. His novel *East of Eden* is primarily based on his grandfather's life in Salinas.

10 medium carrots, sliced
   on diagonal, about
   1/4 inch thin
4 tablespoons butter
1 teaspoon fresh or dry
   tarragon
1/2 teaspoon sugar
1/2 cup Madeira wine

Saute carrots over medium heat in butter for 2 to 3 minutes. Sprinkle with sugar and tarragon. Add Madeira and simmer covered until carrots are tender and wine has evaporated about, 6 to 8 minutes.

Serves six to eight.

Rosemary Glazed Carrots

6 to 8 medium size
   carrots, peeled
1 1/2 cups chicken
   stock or water
2 tablespoon white wine
1/2 teaspoon salt
1/4 teaspoon white
   pepper
3 tablespoons butter
1 1/2 tablespoons fresh
   squeezed lemon juice
1 tablespoon brown sugar
1 1/2 teaspoon fresh
   rosemary,
   finely chopped

Trim carrots, peel and cut into 1/2 inch rounds. In sauce-pan, combine stock, wine and salt. Heat until boiling and add carrot slices. Cook uncovered over high heat 7 to 8 minutes or until tender. Drain and add salt, pepper, butter, lemon juice, brown sugar and rosemary. Toss lightly to coat and cook over low heat, stirring or tossing constantly, until ingredients combine and sugar caramelizes. Remove to serving dish.

Serves six.

Broccoli Cheddar Pie

Cheese Crust
1 cup grated
   Cheddar cheese
3/4 cup flour
1/2 teaspoon salt
1/4 teaspoon dry mustard
1/4 cup melted butter

Filling
1 medium onion,
   chopped
1/4 pound fresh
   mushrooms, sliced
2 tablespoons butter
2 tablespoons flour
1 cup light cream
1 teaspoon salt
1/4 teaspoon nutmeg
2 cups fresh broccoli,
   chopped and cooked
   until tender
3 eggs, slightly beaten
dash of pepper

Preheat oven to 400°. To prepare the cheese crust, combine cheese with flour, seasonings and melted butter. Press on bottom and sides of 10 inch pie pan.

To prepare the filling, saute onions and mushrooms in the butter in a skillet over medium high heat until the mushrooms have given off their liquid and onions are soft. Stir in flour and cook until blond. Add cream, salt, nutmeg and pepper and simmer for 1 minute. Remove from heat and add the cooked broccoli and beaten eggs, stirring well to blend . Pour into the unbaked cheese crust. Bake at 400° for 15 minutes. Reduce heat to 375° and bake for another 20 to 25 minutes.

Serves six.

Sea and Valley Broccoli

Dressing

4 anchovy filets
3 cloves garlic
3 tablespoons lemon juice
1 8 ounce jar sundried
    tomatoes, drained
1/3 cup olive oil
1/3 cup freshly grated
    Parmesan cheese
2 pounds broccoli
    spears trimmed
    to 4-inch lengths

In a food processor using the steel blade, process the anchovy filets, garlic, tomatoes and lemon juice. Add the olive oil in a thin stream and process until smooth. Mix in the Parmesan cheese. Steam or microwave the broccoli until crisp but tender. Drain the broccoli and toss with the dressing. Serve at once.

Serves six.

"His sympathies always go out to the oppressed, the misfits, and the distressed."

– Secretary of the Swedish Academy on awarding the 1962 Nobel Prize for Literature to John Steinbeck

Thai Asparagus

1 pound fresh asparagus
1 ounce dried Chinese
    black mushrooms
    (available in Oriental
    specialty markets,
    sometimes labeled
    "black fungus")
2 tablespoons oil
2 cloves garlic, minced
3 tablespoons
    oyster sauce
1 small red chili pepper,
    seeded and sliced
salt to taste

Rinse asparagus and trim stems. Soak Chinese mushrooms in warm water for 15 minutes. Drain mushrooms and discard stems. Leave the mushrooms whole or slice into 1 inch strips.

Heat oil in a skillet or wok, add garlic and cook until almost golden. Stir in mushrooms and cook, stirring constantly, for 1 minute. Add asparagus, oyster sauce and chili pepper. Stir fry for 3-5 minutes, tasting for salt. Serve immediately.

Serves four.

Marinated Baby Asparagus with Red Bell Pepper

1 pound baby asparagus, stems trimmed

Marinade
1/4 cup fresh lemon juice
1/4 cup tarragon white wine vinegar
1/4 teaspoon ground cloves
1/4 teaspoon ground ginger
1/4 teaspoon dried coriander
1/4 teaspoon dried rosemary
1/4 teaspoon dried tarragon
1 clove garlic, finely chopped
1/4 teaspoon salt and pepper
1/4 cup olive oil
1 red bell pepper, thinly sliced for garnish

Bring a skillet of water to a boil. Add asparagus in a single layer. Cover and cook 4 to 5 minutes. The asparagus should remain bright green and slightly crisp. Drain well and set aside.

To prepare marinade, combine lemon juice, vinegar, garlic and spices in a large bowl. Whisk in olive oil until emulsified. Place asparagus in a loaf pan or other narrow pan. Pour marinade over asparagus and toss to coat. Cover and marinate in refrigerator 30 minutes. Drain and arrange on serving platter or plates. Garnish, laying red bell pepper slices crosswise over the asparagus.

Serves three to four.

Braised Celery
with Walnuts

1 head celery, sliced
   diagonally into
   1 to 1 1/2 inch slices
2 tablespoons butter
1 small onion,
   finely chopped
1/3 cup walnuts,
   coarsely chopped
zest of 1 lemon,
   cut into strips
salt and pepper to taste

Bring 3 cups salted water to a boil. Place celery in a sauce-pan. Add just enough of the boiling water to cover the vegetable. Par boil for 5 minutes. Drain. Melt the butter in a large frying pan. Add onion, walnuts and saute briefly. Add lemon zest, celery, salt and pepper. Toss and heat through.

Serves four.

Artichokes Medley

25 baby artichokes
4 slices bacon, chopped
3/4 cup onion, chopped
3/4 cup celery, chopped
3/4 cup carrots, chopped
2 tablespoons olive oil,
    as needed

Trim top 1/3 of artichokes and remove stems. Plunge artichokes into 2 quarts of boiling water and blanch about 4 minutes. Drain well, and set aside.

Cook chopped bacon and chopped veggies in dutch oven over medium heat until bacon is crisp and veggies are soft. Add artichokes and enough oil to coat artichokes. Cook very slowly for approximately 1 hour. Can be served hot or cold.

Serves ten.

W*hoever ate the first artichoke had to have been very hungry. The lengthy process of peeling off the leaves one by one, then scraping them with your teeth seems an anathema in today's world of fast food. The thistle, related to the sunflower family, produces approximately $29 million for growers each year. As one wit stated, "It's the only vegetable that you have more left of on your plate after you finish eating than before you started."*

Brussels Sprouts in Dilled Walnut Sauce

1 to 1 1/2 pounds fresh
    brussels sprouts,
    left whole or split
    lengthwise
1/2 cup scallions
3 tablespoons fresh
    parsley
2 tablespoons fresh dill
3 tablespoons lemon juice
4 ounces walnuts
4 tablespoons butter,
    softened
salt and pepper to taste

Prepare brussels sprouts and steam until tender. Drain and transfer to a bowl. In a food processor or blender, combine scallions, parsley, dill, lemon juice, walnuts and butter. Blend until smooth. Pour dressing over hot brussels sprouts. Toss and taste for seasonings.

Serves six.

*Historic Adobe,
Monterey*

Belgian Beef Stew

*The First
Brick House,
Monterey*

*Kelp Forest,
Monterey Bay
Aquarium*

Grilled Swordfish with Mango Chili Relish

Montery Bay Aquarium

*Fresh vegetables
from the
Salinas Valley*

Sea & Valley Broccoli

*Fields of
Salinas*

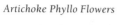

Artichoke Phyllo Flowers

Artichokes
from the
Salinas Valley

Stir-Fried Brussels Sprouts with Basil Sauce

3 pounds brussels sprouts
1/4 cup olive oil
6 cloves garlic, minced
2/3 cup cream
pinch of ground
   red pepper
1/4 teaspoon
   ground nutmeg
salt and pepper to taste
1/2 cup shredded
   fresh basil
1/2 cup freshly grated
   Parmesan cheese

Trim the brussels sprouts; slice evenly through the root end, obtaining about 6 slices from each brussels sprout. Set aside. Heat the olive oil over medium high heat in large skillet. Add the brussels sprouts and saute until sprouts are barely tender, about 5 minutes. Pour in cream and season with red pepper, nutmeg, salt and pepper. Cook until cream is slightly thickened, approximately 2 to 3 minutes. Stir in basil and sprinkle with Parmesan cheese. Serve at once. Makes a delicious side dish with holiday meals – even confirmed brussels sprout-haters are converted!

Serves eight to ten.

Layered Vegetable Terrine

2 pounds ground
  cooked ham
1/2 cup mayonnaise
3 eggs, slightly beaten
2 tablespoons lemon juice
1/4 teaspoon black pepper
1 cup cooked
  spinach, squeezed
  of excess water
5 thick carrots, sliced and
  cooked until tender
1 14 ounce can artichoke
  hearts, drained
  and halved
1 1/2 cups fresh
  tomato sauce, at room
  temperature

Preheat oven to 325°. Combine ham, mayonnaise, eggs, lemon juice and pepper. Mix well. Spread 3/4 cup ham mixture into bottom of lightly oiled 9x5 inch loaf pan. Arrange spinach over ham, leaving 1/2 inch edge around pan. Spread 1 cup ham mixture over spinach. Top with carrots, leaving edge. Spread 1 1/2 cup ham mixture over carrots. Top with artichokes, leaving an edge. Spread remaining ham over artichokes. Press mixture down firmly. Cover with aluminum foil. Bake at 325° for 1 hour. Uncover and continue baking 30 minutes. Chill overnight. Unmold and garnish. Cut into slices and serve with fresh tomato sauce.

Serves eight to ten.

Grilled Eggplant with Marinara Sauce

1/3 cup chopped
   mushrooms
1/4 cup chopped celery
1/4 cup chopped
   green pepper
1/4 teaspoon chopped
   onion
3 tablespoons olive oil
1 cup tomato sauce
1/2 teaspoon
   dried oregano

1/2 teaspoon salt
1/2 teaspoon dried basil
1 teaspoon crushed or
   chopped garlic
dash of pepper
1 medium eggplant
   (about 1 pound)
1/2 teaspoon garlic salt
Fresh basil sprigs
1/4 cup grated
   Parmesan cheese

In a large skillet over medium heat, saute mushrooms, celery, green pepper and onions in 1 tablespoon olive oil. Add tomato sauce, oregano, basil, garlic, dash of pepper and salt. Bring to boil and simmer 15 to 20 minutes, stirring occasionally. Cut eggplant into 1/2 inch thick slices. Brush eggplant with the other 2 tablespoons of oil. Sprinkle with dash of garlic salt. Grill slices on medium heat of barbecue for 2 minutes on each side, or until crisp and tender. Transfer to serving platter. Top with marinara sauce and garnish with fresh basil. Sprinkle with freshly grated Parmesan cheese.

Serves four.

Eggplant stuffed with Ratatouille

The Gold Rush of 1850 made few miners rich, but brought great wealth to an Italian tinsmith, Alberto Trescony. After arriving in Monterey in 1842, Trescony made a meager living fashioning tin cups from cast off tin cans. When gold fever hit, he wisely switched to making tin pans for the miners, selling them for $35 a piece.

Saving his money, Trescony bought Rancho Tularcitos, as well as the Washington Hotel in Monterey and the Halfway House in what would become Salinas.

1/3 cup diced zucchini
3 baby or Japanese eggplants
3 tablespoons olive oil
1/2 cup minced onion
1/2 cup minced red pepper
1 cup canned tomatoes, drained and chopped
2 garlic cloves, minced
1 teaspoon minced fresh thyme or 1/4 teaspoon dried thyme
2 teaspoons minced fresh basil or 1/2 teaspoon dried basil
3 teaspoons minced parsley leaves
3 tablespoons Parmesan cheese

Lightly salt the zucchini and let stand for 30 minutes on paper towels. Pat dry rubbing off the salt. Preheat oven to 400°. Cut the eggplants lengthwise in half and place cut side down on a greased baking pan. Brush with 1 tablespoon oil and bake in 400° oven for 10 minutes. Transfer to a rack and let cool. Scoop out the pulp, leaving 1/4-inch shells. Chop the pulp. Saute the onion and red pepper in 2 tablespoons of olive oil until soft. Add the eggplant pulp and zucchini and cook for 2 to 3 minutes. Add the tomatoes, garlic and herbs to the cooked mixture. Cook over low heat for about 10 minutes, stirring occasionally. Mound the stuffing in the eggplant shells and sprinkle with the parsley and Parmesan cheese. Place in an oiled baking dish and bake for 7 minutes at 350° or until heated through.

Serves six.

Trescony Ratatouille

1 eggplant, cut into
   1 inch cubes
2 tablespoons olive oil
2 onions, chopped
2 crook neck or
   yellow summer squash,
   chopped
1 zucchini, chopped
1 green pepper, chopped
2 cloves garlic, minced
4 tomatoes, coarsely
   chopped

1 6 ounce can tomato
   paste or puree
1 teaspoon dried basil
1/2 teaspoon dried
   tarragon
1/4 teaspoon dried thyme
1/2 lemon
1 tablespoon finely
   chopped parsley
1/4 cup grated
   Parmesan cheese

In a large skillet over medium heat saute eggplant, onions, zucchini, summer squash, bell pepper and garlic in oil until soft. Add tomatoes, seasoning and puree and bring to a boil. Reduce heat and simmer for 30 minutes. Squeeze on a dash of lemon before serving and sprinkle with Parmesan cheese and parsley.

Serves four.

While money may not buy happiness, it did buy Trescony his true love. He had lost his heart to Catherine Cotton Rainey, a New Zealand native who returned his love but unfortunately was already married. She was desperately unhappy with her abusive husband. Finally, her husband agreed to release her from the marriage in return for a large sum of money from Trescony.

The happy couple purchased Rancho San Lucas in the Salinas Valley, where they raised their family.

Crookneck Squash Au Gratin

2 1/2 pounds yellow
   crookneck squash
1 cup grated onion
2 cups grated
   Cheddar cheese
2 eggs, lightly beaten
2 cloves garlic, minced
1/2 teaspoon
   grated nutmeg
salt and pepper to taste
1 cup fresh bread crumbs,
   plus 3 tablespoons
   held in reserve
3 tablespoons butter

Preheat oven to 350º. Cut squash into 1 inch pieces and steam approximately 20 minutes. Drain and puree with wooden spoon. In large bowl, combine squash and other ingredients (except for butter and 3 tablespoons of bread crumbs). Place in buttered 2 quart souffle dish or casserole, dot with butter and sprinkle with remaining bread crumbs. Bake at 350º degrees for 25 minutes.

Serves eight.

Winter Squash

4 medium sized zucchini,
   sliced
4 small yellow crookneck
   squash, sliced
salt, as needed
1 large green pepper,
   sliced
1 yellow onion, thinly
   sliced
1 basket cherry tomatoes,
   cut in half
1 cup grated
   Parmesan cheese
1/2 teaspoon cayenne
   pepper
1 tablespoon vegetable oil

Preheat oven to 350°. Slice the squash and arrange in a single layer and lightly salt. Let stand for at least 30 minutes and pat dry, rubbing off the salt. In a skillet over medium heat, lightly cook the pepper and onion in the oil and transfer to a 3 quart pyrex baking dish. Cut the tomatoes in half. Add all the ingredients to the pyrex dish and lightly toss. Bake at 350° for 20 minutes.

Serves six to eight.

Steinbeck's success came from writing about the plight of the migrant farm workers needed to gather the bounty of the Salinas fields. His first success was Tortilla Flat *in 1935. The books that followed presented a grim look at life.* In Dubious Battle *(1936) is the tragic story of a young labor organizer.* Of Mice and Men *(1937) tells of the barren lives and shattered dreams of two itinerant farm workers.* Their Blood is Strong *(1939) is a nonfictional account of the conditions in the camps of the migrant farm workers.*

Corral de Tierra Zucchini

3 medium zucchini
1 1/2 - 2 tablespoons
 olive oil
1 green pepper, finely
 chopped
2 tomatoes, peeled,
 seeded, and chopped
1 onion, minced
2 cloves garlic, minced
1/4 cup minced parsley
1 teaspoon oregano
salt and pepper
1 cup grated jack cheese
3 slices sourdough bread,
 toasted and broken
 into crumbs

Par boil zucchini until just tender. Cut in half lengthwise. Scoop out zucchini pulp to leave shell. In a large skillet over medium heat, saute onion and garlic in the olive oil until softened. Add zucchini pulp, green pepper, tomatoes, parsley, oregano, salt and pepper. Turn down heat and cook until thickened, about 10 minutes. Taste for seasoning. Fill zucchini shells with mixture. Top with jack cheese and bread crumbs. Broil until tops are bubbly and golden, about 3 minutes.

Black Beans Cilantro

1 pound dry black beans
2 quarts chicken stock
1/4 cup olive oil
1 onion, chopped
5 cloves garlic, chopped
2 fresh hot chilies,
    seeded and chopped
1/4 cup fresh parsley,
    chopped
1/2 cup fresh cilantro,
    chopped

Rinse dried black beans with cold water in strainer. In large stock pot, combine chicken stock, beans and olive oil. Slow boil until stock starts to turn black, approximately 2 hours. Add onion, garlic, chilies, parsley and cilantro. Continue to slow boil until beans are tender and stock is slightly thick.

Serve with a combination of sour cream, grated Monterey Jack and Cheddar cheese, salsa and chopped cilantro. Wonderful as a side dish or serve with flour tortillas and fresh salad as a distinctive main course.

Serves six.

Green Beans with Tomatoes and Mushrooms

2 1/2 pounds fresh green
   beans, cut diagonally
   into 2-inch slices
4 large tomatoes,
   peeled and seeded,
   cut in wedges
7 tablespoons butter
1 large onion, chopped
1/2 pound mushrooms,
   sliced

3 cloves garlic, minced
1 1/4 teaspoon dry basil
1 1/4 teaspoon dry
   oregano leaves
salt to taste
1 cup bread crumbs
1/4 cup grated
   Parmesan cheese

Preheat oven to 400°. Steam beans until tender-crisp, about 4 to 6 minutes. Rinse in cold water and drain. Melt 4 tablespoons butter in wide frying pan over medium high heat. Add onions, mushrooms and 2 cloves of minced garlic. Cook, stirring until soft. Stir in 1 teaspoon basil, oregano and salt. Combine mushroom mixture with beans and tomatoes. Transfer to a shallow 3 quart baking dish. Melt remaining butter in a small pan. Stir in remaining garlic, bread crumbs, cheese, 1/4 teaspoon basil and oregano. Sprinkle crumb mixture over beans. Cover and bake at 400° for 20 minutes or until hot throughout.

Serves ten.

Savory Green Beans with Shallots

In 1964, John Steinbeck was awarded the Presidential Medal of Freedom by Lyndon B. Johnson.

4 slices lean bacon
1/2 cup shallots or
   white part of green
   onion, minced
2 tablespoons herb
   vinegar, such as
   tarragon
1 teaspoon Dijon mustard
1 pound fresh green
   beans, cut French
   style (on the diagonal)
salt and pepper to taste
2 tablespoons chives,
   chopped

In a skillet, fry the bacon until crisp. Drain on paper towel, then crumble into small bits. Saute the shallots or onion in the bacon fat until tender, but not browned. Stir in the vinegar and mustard and set aside. Cook the beans in boiling water for 5-6 minutes until tender. Drain well. Add the beans to the skillet and toss well. Season with salt and pepper to taste. Sprinkle with the reserved bacon and chopped chives. Serve warm.

Serves four.

Whipped Potatoes Potrero

2 pounds russet potatoes
1 cup chicken stock,
    heated
6 tablespoons olive oil
3/4 cup grated
    Parmesan cheese
1/2 teaspoon minced
    garlic
1/2 cup chopped
    fresh chives
salt and pepper to taste

Boil potatoes until tender. Drain and peel. Transfer potatoes to large bowl. Add 3/4 cup hot broth and mix with electric beater until smooth. Gradually beat in oil, garlic and cheese, adding more broth if very thick. Stir in chives. Season with salt and pepper. Garnish with additional cheese.

Serves four.

Papas Harneadas

3 medium onions,
   thinly sliced
4 tablespoons butter
2 tablespoons oil
3-4 medium potatoes,
   peeled and thinly
   sliced
salt and pepper to taste
1 bay leaf
1 1/2 - 2 cups beef
   or veal stock
2 teaspoons thyme

Preheat oven to 375°. Put onions in roasting pan with 2 tablespoons butter and 2 tablespoons oil. Place in oven. Cook until color is light gold, being careful not to burn. Can also be done on stove top while slicing potatoes.

In same roasting pan or large casserole dish, arrange onions in layers with potatoes, seasoning each layer with salt, pepper and thyme. Cover with stock, just to height of potatoes. Add crumbled bay leaf. Dot with butter. Bake for 1 to 1 1/4 hours until tender and well browned. During cooking, press down the top layer of potatoes if they start to curl. The potatoes should be tender and moist when cooked, not wet. Potatoes on top should be crispy.

Serves eight.

Okie Potatoes

In gathering information for Their Blood is Strong, Steinbeck was inspired to write a fictional account of the American migrant farm workers struggling for dignity in the face of oppression. The result was The Grapes of Wrath. The book, published in 1939, was quickly followed by Steinbeck's screenplay for the 1950 movie starring Henry Fonda, and both brought the plight of the dispossessed "Okies" to the attention of the world. The book won a Pulitzer Prize in 1940.

6 medium red new
   potatoes
4 tablespoons butter, or
   more if needed
1/2 cup grated
   Parmesan cheese
1/4 cup dry vermouth

Preheat oven to 350°. Slice potatoes thinly. Place in bottom of buttered casserole. Dot generously with butter. Sprinkle with parmesan. Repeat layers as needed. Pour vermouth over top layer. Bake until golden brown and bubbly, about 30 minutes.

Serves four to six.

Potato and Mushroom Gratin

2 pounds russet
  potatoes, scrubbed
4 slices bacon, chopped
3/4 pound mushrooms,
  thinly sliced
1 onion, thinly sliced
3 cloves of garlic, minced
1 tablespoon chopped
  fresh rosemary
  or 1 teaspoon dry
  rosemary

1 tablespoon minced
  parsley
1/4 teaspoon paprika
pepper to taste
1/4 cup butter, cut
  into 1/4 inch slices
1/2 pound gruyere
  or fontina cheese,
  shredded
3/4 cup chicken stock

Boil potatoes over high heat, 20-30 minutes. Drain and cool. Cut into 1/4 inch thick slices, leaving skins on. Preheat oven to 425°. Over medium heat in 12 inch fry pan, cook bacon until crisp. Remove and drain bacon. Discard all but 2 tablespoons fat. Add mushrooms, onion, garlic, rosemary and parsley. Cook about 10 minutes, until mushrooms have released their liquid and onion has softened and is lightly golden. Stir in bacon, paprika and pepper. Place in 2 quart baking dish. Layer 1/2 the potatoes, 1/2 the butter, 1/2 the mushroom mixture and 1/2 the cheese. Repeat, ending with cheese. Pour stock evenly over all. Bake at 425° for 30-35 minutes.

Serves eight to ten.

Roasted Garlic Mashed Potatoes

2 heads garlic, papery
  outer skin removed,
  cloves intact
  and unpeeled
2 teaspoons olive oil
8 large potatoes, peeled
  and quartered
1/2 cup unsalted butter,
  softened

1 1/2 cups half and half
2 teaspoons salt
1/2 teaspoon freshly
  ground pepper
1/4 cup chopped mixed
  fresh herbs (parsley,
  sage, rosemary,thyme)
  or 1 teaspoon dried
  of each

Preheat oven to 400°. Place garlic heads on sheet of aluminum foil; drizzle with olive oil. Wrap tightly; bake 1 hour or until softened. Remove from oven; cool. Squeeze garlic paste from each unpeeled clove into large bowl; set aside.

Bring a large stock pot of water to a boil. Add potatoes and reduce heat. Simmer 20 minutes or until potatoes are tender. Drain. Return potatoes to pan. Over low heat, heat potatoes 3 to 5 minutes, shaking pan constantly to dry potatoes. Add potatoes to garlic. With potato masher, puree potatoes. Add butter and mash until blended. Continue mashing potato mixture until creamy, adding half and half gradually. Mix in salt, pepper and herbs.

Serves ten.

PIZZA, PASTA, & RISOTTO

Big Sur

The area encourages individualism. "Do your own thing," is the rallying cry of Big Sur, where the Santa Lucia Mountains tumble into the surf of the Crystal blue Pacific. The rugged remoteness of the area attracted settlers who tackled the environment on their own terms. Later, guests at Esalen Institute or the Ventana Inn would examine their existence in the world and their relation to the extraordinary beauty of their surroundings.

Whatever the attraction, this rugged Monterey Coast brings out the different drummer in everyone. So pull the record album from the back of the stack, put on your oldest blue jeans, and encounter the experience of Big Sur.

Rotolo

1/2 basic pasta recipe
2 pounds spinach,
   washed and stemmed
2 pounds Ricotta cheese
2 eggs, lightly beaten
1 teaspoon nutmeg,
   freshly grated
1/2 teaspoon salt
1/2 teaspoon pepper

1 cup grated
   Parmesan cheese
1 egg, well beaten
12 pieces proscuitto
cheesecloth and string
1 cup butter, melted
fresh basil leaves
   as garnish

Basic Pasta Recipe

4 1/4 cups unsifted
   all-purpose flour
2 teaspoons salt
3 eggs, beaten
1/4 cup lukewarm water
1 tablespoon olive oil

To make basic pasta recipe, process all ingredients together in food processor until ball of dough is formed. Knead on floured surface. Cover and let rest 30 minutes.

Enjoy this basic recipe for all your fresh pasta needs.

Makes 1 1/2 pounds.

Cook spinach in boiling water for 5 minutes. Cool, drain and squeeze out as much moisture as possible. Chop spinach finely in food processor. Mix spinach with Ricotta, 2 eggs, nutmeg, salt, pepper and Parmesan.

To assemble, roll out dough from basic pasta recipe to a paper-thin 20 inch square. Cut dough in half. On each, spread spinach/cheese filling leaving 1 inch uncovered on all sides. Brush uncovered dough edges with remaining well beaten egg. Layer proscuitto over cheese filling. Fold in long edges on each piece and roll up like jelly roll. You will have 2 10-inch rolls. Wrap each in cheesecloth, tie at 3 places and put rolls in boiling water in roasting pan. Cook uncovered for 10 minutes. Let stand in cooking water 30 minutes longer. Remove and chill while still wrapped.

To serve, preheat oven to 400°. Remove cheesecloth and cut rolls into 1/2 inch thick slices. Arrange slices (overlapping each other) in a shallow baking pan and spoon melted butter over slices. Bake at 400° 10 to 15 minutes until hot. Serve with additional brown butter and basil leaves. Easy to make ahead and attractive as both a main course or an appetizer.

Serves eight to ten.

Mussels and Scallops on Linguini

1/2 pound salmon
1 tablespoon olive oil
4 cloves garlic, crushed
3 large shallots, minced
1 pound mussels in
    shell, scrubbed
    and debearded
1 pound scallops
1/4 cup chopped fresh
    basil leaves
1/4 cup chopped
    fresh parsley

1 cup dry white wine
1/2 teaspoon salt
1 teaspoon white pepper
1 pound linguini,
    cooked according to
    directions on package
1/2 cup grated
    Romano cheese
1/2 cup grated
    Parmesan cheese

In 1 cup of water, steam salmon until meat flakes and can easily be removed from the bones. Remove fish and reserve water.

In large sauce pan, saute olive oil, garlic and shallots over medium high heat. Add water from salmon and wine; bring to a boil. Add mussels and scallops. Steam until mussels have opened and scallops are opaque, approximately 5 minutes. Add basil, parsley, deboned salmon and pepper. Cook for an additional 5 minutes. Mix in pasta and stir in cheeses.

Serves six to eight as an appetizer.

Scallop Lasagna

2 pounds bay scallops
6 tablespoons butter
1 cup chopped
green onion
3 cloves garlic, crushed
1 teaspoon fresh thyme
leaves or 1/2
teaspoon dried thyme
1/3 cup flour

1 cup chicken stock
1 cup whipping cream
1/2 cup dry white
vermouth
1/2 pound dry
lasagna noodles
2 cups grated
Muenster cheese
1 cup grated Swiss cheese

Preheat oven to 350°. Rinse scallops well and drain. Melt 1 tablespoon of butter in 12 inch frying pan. Add onion, garlic and thyme. Saute over medium high heat for 1 minute. Add scallops and cook, stirring often until opaque in center, 2 to 3 minutes. Strain scallops for 20 minutes, reserving juices.

In same frying pan, melt remaining butter on medium heat. Add flour and stir until it turns lightly golden. Remove from heat and mix in stock, cream and vermouth. Return to high heat and bring to a boil, stirring constantly until thickened. Set aside.

Cook lasagna noodles until tender to bite, about 10 minutes. Drain. Rinse lasagna with cold water. Drain and set aside.

Pour scallop juices into a 1 to 1 1/2 quart pan and boil on high heat, uncovered, until reduced to about 2 tablespoons. Stir to keep juices from scorching. Mix juices with cream sauce. Line the bottom of a 9x12 inch buttered baking pan with 1/3 of the lasagna noodles. Pour sauce over entire mixture. Spread noodles with 1/3 of the grated cheese. Repeat layers twice more ending with cheese on top. Top with 1/3 of scallops. Cover with foil. Bake at 350° for 20 minutes. Remove foil and bake until cheese is golden, about 20 more minutes. Let stand 15 minutes before cutting.

*T*ravel down the Big Sur Coast was rough. In the 1860s, the rough wagon road from Monterey ran only as far as the present day Highlands Inn. From there, a small trail wound around for several miles until it disappeared into the wild brush near the Post property. The southward trek in search of land was treacherous in covered wagons, accompanied by cattle, horses, goats and other livestock. Once there, the trip north to shop in Monterey could take three to four days.

Fettuccine Portofino

2 tablespoons
  chopped garlic
2 tablespoons olive oil
2 cups fresh tomatoes,
  diced
2 ounces or 1/4 cup
  tomato paste
1 teaspoon oregano
1 cup half and half
2 dozen prawns, peeled
  and deveined
  (26-30 count)

1 pound bay scallops
1 pound mussels,
  scrubbed
  and debearded
1 dozen clams in shell,
  scrubbed
1 pound fettuccine,
  cooked according to
  directions on package
1/4 cup grated
  Parmesan cheese

In large skillet, saute garlic in olive oil. Add fresh tomatoes, tomato paste and oregano. Stir well. Add half and half and heat until thickened. Add prawns and scallops. Cook 5 to 7 minutes, stirring so as not to boil. In a large saucepan, steam mussels and clams in boiling water until just opened. In large pasta dish, place hot drained fettuccine. Pour skillet mixture over pasta. Mix well. Add drained mussels and clams. Top with grated Parmesan cheese.

Serves four.

Three-Colored Pasta with Peppers

Tomato Basil Sauce
1/4 cup olive oil
1/2 cup minced onion
2 garlic cloves, minced
1/4 cup chopped fresh
   basil leaves
1 teaspoon salt
3 pounds tomatoes,
   peeled, seeded
   and chopped
1/4 teaspoon ground
   pepper

Sauteed Peppers
1/4 cup olive oil
2 red bell peppers, seeded
and cut in julienne strips

1 yellow bell pepper,
   seeded and cut in
   julienne strips
2 garlic cloves, minced
1 large handful of fresh
   basil leaves, cut into
   long thin strips

1/2 pound spinach
   linguine
1/2 pound egg linguine
1/2 pound tomato
   linguine
1/2 cup grated Parmesan
   cheese
basil sprigs for garnish

To prepare the tomato basil sauce, cook onions in olive oil over low heat about 8 minutes until translucent. Add garlic and cook 30 seconds. Increase heat to medium and add remaining ingredients. Bring to a boil and reduce heat. Simmer 25 minutes until most of the liquid is evaporated.

While linguine is cooking according to directions on package, saute peppers in olive oil over medium heat for about 10 minutes or until no longer crisp. Add garlic and cook 30 seconds. Add basil. Toss drained pasta with peppers and top with tomato sauce. Garnish with fresh Parmesan and basil.

Serves six.

Although it may not seem like cattle country, the pioneers of Big Sur were drawn to the remote area because grazing land was available at the right price - free. In return for 160 acres with a million dollar view, a family had to live on the land for five years, according to the Homestead Act of 1862.

William Brainard Post, Michael and Barbara Pfeiffer, John and Laura Partington, Gabriel and Elizabeth Dani, and Wilbur Harlan all homesteaded along the Big Sur Coast and increased the families' holdings when the sons filed claims on adjacent property.

Point Sur Pasta

1 pound penne or
   other short pasta
1 1/2 tablespoons olive oil
2 cloves garlic, minced
1 small fresh chili,
   minced or 1 teaspoon
   dried pepper flakes
1 cauliflower, broken
   into florets
8 ounces canned Italian
   plum tomatoes
1 cup chicken stock
1 cup cream
1/4 cup grated Asiago
   or Parmesan cheese

In large skillet, heat olive oil and add the chopped garlic and the fresh chili pepper. (If using the pepper flakes, add when adding stock.) Cook over low heat for about 3 minutes, being careful not to burn the garlic. Add cauliflower florets to pan. Cook for 5 minutes, then add the tomatoes and their juice. Simmer for 10 minutes and then add the stock. Cook until cauliflower is tender.

Cook the pasta according to directions on package.

Add the cream to the cauliflower mixture. Mash the cauliflower with a potato masher or pulse gently in food processor. Sauce should still be slightly chunky. Drain pasta and stir in the sauce. Garnish with grated Asiago or fresh Parmesan cheese.

Serves four.

Pasta del Lobos

2 tablespoons olive oil
1 pound sweet or hot
    Italian sausage, cut in
    one inch slices
1 cup thinly sliced
    red onion
2 red bell peppers, cored,
    seeded and cut into
    thin strips
8 cloves garlic, finely
    chopped
1/4 cup dry white wine
2 tablespoons chopped
    fresh basil or 1 tea-
    spoon dried sweet basil
1 teaspoon dried oregano
salt and pepper to taste
1 pound pasta of choice,
    cooked according to
    package directions

Heat olive oil in a wide skillet and cook sausage until browned. Remove sausage and drain on paper towels. Drain all but 2 tablespoons of oil from skillet. Add onions to pan and saute over medium heat for about 5 minutes. Raise heat, add peppers to pan and saute 3 or 4 minutes. Add garlic and cook for 1 or 2 additional minutes. Return cooked sausage slices to pan, add the wine and cook 2 to 3 more minutes to reduce the wine slightly. Add herbs, salt and pepper to taste. Serve over freshly cooked pasta.

Serves six.

With Europe engulfed in the beginnings of world war, author Henry Miller was forced out of his writer's haven in the Greek islands in 1942 and settled in the Partington Ridge area of Big Sur. There, the author of _The Tropic of Cancer_ and _The Rosy Crucifixion_ , joined other artists seeking a haven from the social atmosphere of the colony at Carmel-by-the-Sea. These artists were inspired by the silence of the forests and the loneliness of the coast.

Garlic and Ginger Shrimp with Angel Hair Pasta

2 tablespoons peanut oil
2 cloves garlic, minced
1 inch ginger root, peeled and grated
1/3 pound fresh shrimp, peeled and deveined
1 can sliced water chestnuts
1 carrot, grated
1/2 green bell pepper, julienned
3 to 4 tablespoons soy sauce
1/2 red bell pepper, julienned
4 ounces angel hair pasta, cooked according to package directions
cilantro to garnish

In non-stick skillet or wok, saute garlic and ginger in oil over medium high heat until golden brown. Add shrimp and saute until cooked through. Add all vegetables, mix, then add soy sauce. Continue cooking, stirring constantly, until vegetables are warm. Serve over angel hair pasta. May be garnished with cilantro.

This is a very light dish which can be extended to serve four to six by using more pasta or shrimp or vegetables.

Serves two.

Pasta con Sugo Fresco

4 pounds ripe
   roma tomatoes
1 small carrot, cut
   into chunks
1 celery stalk, cut
   into chunks
2 cloves garlic
2 tablespoons fresh
   sweet basil
1/2 small yellow onion,
   peeled and cut
   into chunks

2 to 3 tablespoons
   olive oil
1 teaspoon sugar
salt and pepper to taste
3/4 pound pasta of
   choice, cooked
   according to directions
   on package
grated Parmesan cheese

Parboil tomatoes for 2 to 3 minutes. Meanwhile, place carrot, celery, garlic, basil and onion in food processor and puree. In a 3 quart saucepan, saute pureed mixture in olive oil until softened, about 4 minutes.

Half or quarter parboiled tomatoes. Push tomato pieces a few at a time through a sieve or food mill to remove seeds and skin. Combine tomato pulp with pureed mixture and add sugar, salt and pepper to taste. Cook on medium low heat for about 20 minutes. Pour cooked sauce over boiled pasta. Serve with grated Parmesan cheese.

Serves four.

> *"If the soul were to choose an arena in which to stage its agonies, this would be the place for it. One feels so exposed – not only to the elements, but to the sight of God."*
>
> *– Henry Miller*
> *about the Big Sur Coast*

Pasta della Madre di Diavolo

1 pound penne pasta
Salt
1/3 cup extra virgin
   olive oil
2 tablespoons
   crushed garlic
2 scallions, chopped
   finely
1 bay leaf
5 sprigs fresh thyme
1 1/2 cups hot coppacola
   (pork shoulder
   butt), diced or cut in
   thin strips

1 cup fresh jalapeno
   peppers, seeded and
   finely chopped
1/3 cup dry red wine
1 pound raw shrimp,
   deveined,
   tails left intact
1/2 cups grated Parmesan
   or Pecorino cheese
Fresh ground black
   pepper to taste
4 tablespoons chopped
   parsley

Boil penne in salted water until it is "al dente," drain and set aside.

Heat olive oil at medium temperature in a large saucepan. Add garlic, scallions and herbs. Reduce heat and simmer for a few minutes. Add the hot coppacola and simmer for approximately 4 minutes. Add the peppers and red wine. Continue to simmer for another two to three minutes, stirring frequently. Add the shrimp and cook until the shrimp turn pink.

Add the boiled penne to the saucepan, mix and cover. This allows the pasta to absorb the liquids. Empty the pan contents into a large serving dish, mix in Parmesan cheese and fresh ground pepper. Sprinkle with chopped parsley and serve.

Serves four to six.

Eggplant Risotto

2 quarts chicken stock
1 cup dry white wine
2 tablespoons butter
2 tablespoons olive oil
1/2 cup chopped onion
4 cloves minced garlic
1 cup eggplant, cubed
(soaked in cold salt
water for 30
minutes, drained and
patted dry)

1 cup chicken, cubed
1 pound Arborio Riso
(Italian Rice)
1/4 cup chopped
fresh basil
1/2 cup chopped roma
tomatoes
1/2 cup freshly grated
Parmesan cheese

Heat stock and wine together in a saucepan. Bring to a slow boil and reduce heat to keep warm.

Heat butter and olive oil in large heavy skillet on medium high heat. Add onion, garlic, eggplant and chicken. Cook until onion is soft but not brown, about 5 minutes. Remove from pan, leaving oils behind. Add riso and saute quickly, about 1 minute. Over medium heat, add combined stock and wine to riso 1 cup at a time, stirring constantly until stock is absorbed. Repeat with each cup of stock. Continue until stock is used and riso is plump and tender, but still firm to the bite, approximately 30 minutes. During the last 10 minutes of cooking riso, add onion, garlic, eggplant, chicken, basil and tomatoes. Remove from heat and stir in parmesan cheese. Serve immediately.

Serves six.

Called the "Aquarian Think Tank" by *TIME* magazine, Esalen Institute continues to draw thousands seeking inner awareness.

The site, once sacred to the Esalen Indians, was originally called "Tok-i-toc" or "hot healing waters" and became a Big Sur Hot Springs.

In reaction to the unrest of the 1960's, Michael Murphy and partner Richard Price began a series of weekend seminars dedicated to the discovery of the "Human Potential." Thus began the Esalen Institute, devoted to "explore those trends in education, religion, philosophy, and the physical and behavioral sciences which emphasize the potentialities and values of human existence," according to an early catalogue.

Esalen continues to be a favorite place to escape, lay back, and "get in touch with yourself."

Fennel-Pesto Risotto

1/2 cup dry white wine

5 cups chicken stock

2 tablespoons
   unsalted butter

2 tablespoons olive oil

1/3 cup minced onion

1 clove garlic

1 1/2 cup Arborio Riso
   (Italian Rice)

1 tablespoon minced
   fennel leaves

1 cup chopped fennel

2 tablespoons pesto sauce

1/3 cup grated
   Parmesan cheese

Heat wine and chicken stock in medium saucepan over medium heat. In large saucepan, heat butter and 1 tablespoon of olive oil over medium high heat. Add onion and garlic and saute until onion is faintly golden, about 7 to 8 minutes. Add riso to onion mixture and stir quickly. Reduce heat to medium-low and ladle about 1/2 cup of stock into the rice mixture. Stir. Add minced fennel leaves and chopped fennel and continue to stir. Ladle in an additional 1/2 cup stock when previous stock has almost been completely absorbed, about every 2 to 3 minutes. Continue until all stock is absorbed. Add pesto sauce, 1 tablespoon olive oil and Parmesan cheese. Stir.

Serves four.

Risotto Cabrillo

3 cups chicken stock
2 tablespoons butter
1/2 cup chopped
   yellow onion
1 1/2 cups Arborio Riso
   (Italian rice)
3 tablespoons olive oil
3 green onions, chopped
1/3 cup coarsely
   grated zucchini
1/3 cup coarsely
   grated carrots

2 cups chopped
   fresh spinach
3 ripe tomatoes, diced
1 ounce dried porcini
   mushrooms
1 teaspoon dried basil
1/4 cup cream
1/4 cup dry white wine
3/4 cup freshly grated
   Parmesan cheese
salt and pepper to taste

Heat chicken stock to boiling. In separate 2 quart heavy saucepan, melt butter. Saute yellow onion and rice until rice is light tan. Add 1/2 of boiling stock to rice mixture and cover. Cook over low heat for about 10 minutes. Meanwhile, in a large frying pan, heat olive oil and vegetables, including mushrooms over medium heat. Cook until vegetables begin to collapse, about 7 to 8 minutes. Add remaining stock to rice, along with vegetables, basil, cream and wine. Simmer 10 minutes or until most of liquid is absorbed. Stir frequently to prevent sticking. Mix in cheese, salt and pepper.

Serves six.

The full glory of the Big Sur coastline - and the Big Sur spirit - is probably best viewed at the Big Sur Marathon. Athletes from all over the world come to run the windy 26 miles from Big Sur to Carmel, supported by volunteers and well-wishers from all over the Peninsula. As the runners progress, they are welcomed by string quartets and brass bands. Children pass out water at their grandparents' front doors. Hundreds of people participate in a 7 or 10 mile walk as part of the event. At Rio Road, near the Carmel Mission, the atmosphere resembles a fair, as hundreds gather to watch the runners cross the finish line. Exhausting as the climb may be along the coast, the runners return each year drawn by the enthusiastic supporters and the breathtaking views.

Chile Poblano Rice

Poblanos are large, dark-green, heart-shaped chilies with unique flavor. Anaheims could substitute.

Roast chilies under broiler until skin turns black and bubbles. Remove skin, seeds and veins.

2 tablespoons butter
1 cup long grain
   white rice
1 medium red potato,
   unpeeled and diced
1 chili poblano, roasted
   and torn into strips
1 small clove garlic,
   chopped
1/2 small white onion,
   sliced
2 cups chicken stock
salt and pepper to taste

Heat butter in medium saucepan over medium high heat. Add rice, potato, chili, garlic and onion and saute until onions are transparent and rice lightly browned. Cover with chicken stock, reduce heat to simmer, and cover with tight-fitting lid. Let cook until liquid is absorbed, approximately 15 to 20 minutes. Stir and serve.

Serves six.

Deep Dish Garlic Cornbread Pizza

1/2 cup flour
1/2 cup cornmeal
1/2 teaspoon salt
1 teaspoon baking
powder
1/2 cup softened
margarine
1/2 cup Parmesan cheese
2 eggs, well beaten
1/4 cup buttermilk
1 tablespoon olive oil
2/3 cup sliced and
chopped whole green
onions (use tops too)
4 cloves garlic, minced

4 medium mushrooms,
sliced
1 1/2 cups stewed
tomatoes, drained
and chopped
1/4 cup chopped
fresh basil
1 small green bell pepper,
slivered
1 small red bell pepper,
slivered
1 small yellow bell
pepper, slivered
1/2 cup grated
Mozzarella cheese

Preheat oven to 375°. Combine dry ingredients. Reserve. In mixing bowl combine margarine and Parmesan cheese. Add eggs and buttermilk. Mix well. Add flour mixture to egg mixture and blend well. Spoon this mixture into a greased 7x11 inch pan. Set aside.

In a large skillet over medium high heat, saute the onions, garlic and mushrooms quickly in the olive oil for 1 to 2 minutes. Add the chopped stewed tomatoes and cook quickly until the liquid has been absorbed. Cool slightly. Top the cornmeal crust with the tomato mushroom mixture. Sprinkle with fresh basil. Layer on peppers and top with grated Mozzarella.

Bake 30 minutes or until a toothpick comes out clean.

Serves six to eight.

Ventana Big Sur Country Inn Resort is situated on 243 acres, 1200 feet above the Pacific Ocean on the Big Sur Coast, 28 miles south of Carmel. The land upon which Ventana was built was originally owned by the Post family, fourth generation Homesteaders, and was settled by their great-grandfather in 1860. It was built in 1975 by writer Lawrence Spector and aquired by Transamerica Realty Investors in 1980. The buildings were designed by Kipp Stewart of Big Sur. They are of weathered cedar latticed against the sun and dispersed about a mountain meadow among Redwood, Oak and Bay Laurel trees.

Ventana Inn is a well known get-away and treasured by visitors for its soothing atmosphere and recooperative amenities. The inn offers two 4' deep pools. Adjoining the pools are bathhouses containing Japanese Hot Baths and sun decks, one with its own sauna. All of the baths have clothing-optional areas.

Spinach Pizza

Pizza Dough
1 tablespoon sugar
1 cup warm water,
    105°-115°
1 package dry yeast
3 cups unbleached flour
1/4 cup olive oil

Spinach Topping
2 bunches fresh spinach,
    triple washed
1 tablespoon olive oil
6 ounces Feta cheese,
    crumbled
6 to 7 ounces sundried
    tomatoes, packed
    in olive oil, drained
4 tablespoons grated
    Parmesan cheese

To prepare dough, dissolve sugar in warm water, sprinkle yeast over water and let bubble five minutes. Mix flour and olive oil by making a well out of the flour and pouring olive oil into the middle. Add water/yeast mixture slowly, using approximately 3/4 of mixture. Knead until dough-like. Place in a greased bowl, cover and let rise 45 minutes. At this point either use and enjoy, or freeze until needed.

To prepare topping, preheat oven to 500°. In a large skillet over medium-high heat, fry spinach in olive oil until limp. Roll out pizza dough to fit 14 inch pan, flour bottom of pan and lightly oil the top of the dough. Top with spinach. Add Feta cheese and sundried tomatoes. Sprinkle with Parmesan cheese. Bake at 500° for 10 to 12 minutes or until bubbly.

Serves two to four.

Garlic Chicken Pizza

Jeano Abraham
Allegro Gourmet Pizzeria

Garlic Chicken Topping
2 cups chicken breast,
   cooked
3 tablespoons olive oil
1/2 cup diced onion
1/4 cup chopped garlic
6 ounces Mozzarella
   cheese, grated
8 thin slices eggplant

1 cup sliced zucchini
8 ounces mushrooms,
   sliced
1/4 to 1/2 teaspoon dried
   crushed red pepper
1/4 cup sliced almonds
1/4 cup grated Parmesan
   or Romano cheese

Preheat oven to 500°. Cut chicken into cubes and mix with 2 tablespoons olive oil, onions and garlic. Saute lightly in small skillet over medium high heat. Set aside. See Spinach Pizza recipe on page 126 for pizza dough recipe. Roll dough to fit 14 inch pan size and paint with remaining olive oil. Top with Mozzarella cheese, eggplant, zucchini, mushrooms, chicken, red pepper and almonds. Cook 10 to 15 minutes until cheese is melted and crust is golden brown. Sprinkle with Parmesan cheese.

You may also use a prepared pizza crust for this recipe.

Serves two to four.

Allegro has been a winner for locals and visitors for many years. It has been recognized as "Best Pizza" by readers of Coast Weekly. Allegro was also chosen for "Best Takeout" and earned the distinction of "Best Caesar Salad." The American Heart Association named Allegro's cioppino as "Best Entree" in a gourmet competition.

The restaurant's owner, Jeano Abraham, creates a fascinating menu including at least 18 specialty pizzas, most with a special history to enhance the menu. Some of the recipes are from Jeano's family and the ingredients in Allegro's pizza dough remain a secret. In addition to the famous pizzas, Allegro offers pastas, antipasti, sandwiches and wonderful creative salads. All salads are made from mixed greens direct from local farms to add to their freshness.

Allegro Gourmet Pizzeria is located in Pacific Grove and in Carmel.

Zucchini and Tomato Focaccia

Nepenthe, located 28 miles south of Carmel, is one of the most picturesque spots in California. The decks overlook the Pacific Ocean, the Santa Lucia Mountains and a forty mile view of the south coast of Big Sur.

Built on the site of "The Log House," the property was once owned by the old "Trails Club" as well as by Orsen Wells and Rita Hayworth. The land was purchased in 1947 by Bill and Lolly Fassett.

"No individual can own it, it belongs to everyone," said Lolly. Out of the feeling that the site and its magnificent vistas were too vast and wonderful to keep to themselves grew the idea of Nepenthe as an isle of no-care. They sought out Rowan Maiden, a student of Frank Lloyd Wright, to design the timeless structure. Native materials, redwood and adobe, were used so that the building became one with the landscape and the earth on which it stands.

Dough
3 1/2 teaspoons yeast
1 teaspoon sugar
1 3/4 cups warm water
5 1/2 cups bread flour
1 teaspoon salt
5 tablespoons olive oil

Topping
1 1/3 pound zucchini, thinly sliced
1/3 pound roma tomatoes, cored and sliced
1 teaspoon marjoram
3 tablespoons olive oil
2 cups shredded Mozzarella
salt to taste

Mix yeast with sugar in water for 5 minutes, until foamy. Add flour, salt and 3 tablespoons oil, combine and knead 2 minutes until sticky. Place dough in greased bowl, cover and let rise 1 1/2 hours. Punch down and press into greased jelly roll pan. Let rise 1 hour.

While dough is rising, place zucchini, tomato, marjoram and half of oil in baking pan. Bake 20 to 25 minutes at 450° until zucchini is translucent and juices evaporate. Turn once while baking.

Make dimples in dough, spread with remaining oil and Mozzarella. Distribute zucchini mixture over top. Bake at 400° for 35 to 40 minutes. If topping browns before dough, cover with foil. It is very colorful and delicious with pasta or served for lunch with salad.

Serves ten to twelve.

SEAFOOD

Cannery Row

"Fish are in," the cry went out. Bells rang, sirens blared, and hundreds of workers descended on the waterfront area of Monterey known as Cannery Row. Putting sardines in cans was their livelihood. But the fish swam away, the canneries closed, and the workers sought employment elsewhere. The area was abandoned. The area's heyday was remembered only in John Steinbeck's novels.

Cannery Row has undergone a rebirth. The lure of Steinbeck's words, the crash of the ocean, and the sparkle of Monterey Bay now draw a new clientele to the waterfront area. Visitors wander the street, roaming from antique shops and novelty boutiques to the world-famous Monterey Bay Aquarium. And for those who are hungry, the Row's renowned chefs take the freshest catch of the day and send out the new cry, "Fish is on."

Calamari Vinaigrette

3 pounds calamari,
   cleaned
1 green pepper, seeded
   and diced
1 red onion, diced
1 small can pimentos
   or 1 small red
   pepper, minced
6 cloves garlic,
   finely chopped
1/2 bunch parsley,
   finely chopped
3 tablespoons capers,
   drained
salt and pepper to taste
1 cup extra virgin
   olive oil
juice of one lemon
1/4 cup red wine vinegar

How to Clean Calamari

Pull off the heads and pull out the cuttle bone (the hard plastic-like bone in the body). Squeeze out the insides. Cut off the tentacles below the eyes. Discard eyes.

Wash calamari and cut into 1/4 inch rings. Bring a large pot of water to a boil. Add calamari rings. Cook 30 seconds if doing all 3 pounds at once or 15 seconds for a smaller quantity. Drain and refresh in cold water to stop cooking. Pat dry on paper towels. In large bowl mix remaining ingredients. Add calamari, toss and taste for seasoning. Can be served immediately or made a day ahead.

Serves six to eight.

Whaling, often thought of as an East Coast endeavor, was a major industry in Monterey in the latter half of the 19th Century. Whalers, often immigrants from Portugal, hunted the Humpback and the California Grey in Monterey Bay during the animals' yearly migration from Arctic waters to the Sea of Cortez in Baja, California.

Whales were hunted primarily for their blubber, which was rendered into valuable whale oil in try pots on the Monterey beaches. For many years the area's two major whaling companies each produced about 1,000 barrels of oil a year. The bones were used for ladies' corsets, hair combs, silverware handles and local pavement.

Whaling died out in the 1870s as the whales were overhunted and whale oil was replaced by mineral oil for light and lubrication.

The Old Whaling Station and The First Brick House, homes of early Monterey whalers, have been restored for public enjoyment by the Junior League of Monterey County.

Petrale Sole Madeira

*I*t began as China Point. In the 1850's the Chinese began immigrating to Monterey. Often whole families would take up residence along the Pacific Ocean, using ancient methods to begin Monterey's fishing industry.

The Chinese were victims of their own success. Their industrious methods produced fish for their own sustenance, and a bountiful supply for drying and selling. With a purported $200,000 annual business by the end of the century, the Chinese became victims of racial intolerance. The smell of rotten and drying fish also elicited complaints from the newly founded Pacific Grove Retreat Association.

The adaptive Chinese soon began fishing at night for a fish plentiful in the waters but not caught by others - squid.

Monterey's Chinatown was destroyed on May 16, 1906, when flames engulfed the shanty-like settlement, signaling the end of the Chinese fishing industry.

1 large egg
3/4 cup flour
1 1/2 teaspoons salt
1/4 teaspoon pepper
1/4 teaspoon sweet
   paprika
1 1/2 pounds petrale
   sole fillets
1/2 cup butter or
   margarine
3 tablespoons olive oil
1/4 cup madeira
1/4 cup fresh lemon juice
8 lemon slices
1/4 cup small capers,
   drained
1/4 cup minced parsley

Beat the egg slightly in a bowl. On large plate, combine the flour, salt, pepper and paprika. Dip each fillet first in egg and then in flour mixture, shaking off excess. In large skillet, heat the butter and olive oil over moderate heat until hot, but not smoking. Cook the fillets for 3 minutes on each side until golden. Transfer cooked fillets to a warm platter, and pour out all but three tablespoons of fat in the skillet. Add the madeira, and reduce by half. Add lemon juice and return fillets to skillet. Heat with lemon slices on top for 30 seconds. Transfer fillets carefully to platter. Top with sauce, sprinkle with capers and parsley before serving.

Serves four.

Sole Wellington

2 tablespoons butter
1 1/4 cup sliced
   mushrooms
1/2 cup diced shallots
6 green onions, chopped
1/2 cup dry white wine
2 cups bay shrimp,
   cooked and chopped
1/3 cup fresh chopped
   cilantro
1/2 cup whipping cream
2 teaspoons beurre manie
   (1 teaspoon melted
   butter mixed with 1
   teaspoon flour)

parchment paper
butter for pan preparation
6 sole fillets (5 or 6 oz.
   each) lightly salted
salt and ground pepper
   to taste
6 6-inch squares puff
   pastry, rolled to
   1/8-1/4 inch thick
   (2 packages of frozen
   puff pastry sheets)
1 egg, beaten with 1
   tablespoon water

Bernaise Sauce

2 tablespoons tarragon
   vinegar
2 tablespoons dry white wine
1 tablespoon chopped shallots
8 tablespoons butter
3 egg yolks

Combine first three ingredients in a small skillet over medium high heat. Remove skillet from heat and place ingredients in double boiler or place small skillet in larger skillet of boiling water. Whisk in butter and then egg yolks being careful not to cook the egg yolks. Sauce should thicken to consistency of Hollandaise Sauce.

To prepare filling, melt 2 tablespoons butter in sauce pan over medium high heat. Add mushrooms, shallots, and green onion. Saute 6 to 7 minutes. Add wine, increase heat to high and cook, stirring frequently, for about 4 minutes. Add shrimp and cilantro, stirring frequently for 1 minute. Reduce heat and add cream. Gradually add beurre manie, stirring until thickened. Season with salt and pepper. Remove from heat and cool. Can be made 1 day ahead and refrigerated.

Preheat oven 375°. Line baking pan with parchment paper. Butter paper. Spoon 4 tablespoons of filling over each fillet. Roll up securely. Set each rolled fish in center of pastry square. Fold pastry over fish envelope style. Do not overlap pastry by more than 1 inch. Moisten and seal edges with beaten egg. Cover tightly and refrigerate until ready to cook. Brush pastry with remaining egg. Transfer to parchment lined pan. Bake until pastry is golden brown, 20-25 minutes. Spoon Bernaise sauce onto plate and arrange Wellingtons on top.

Serves six.

Grilled Salmon with Fresh Pineapple Salsa

"*Carmel - By - The - Sea, Pacific Grove-By-God, and Monterey-By-The Smell" - this was a local saying in the 1920's referring to the fishy smell eminating from Monterey's Cannery Row. While the canneries smelled only of sweet success to the fishermen and cannery workers, it soured the area's tourist industry. Threats of legal action persuaded Monterey civic leaders to become pioneers in environmental control when the city council passed an ordinance requiring canneries to control the smell of success.*

❦

Salmon Marinade
6 tablespoons butter
1/3 cup honey
1/3 cup dark brown sugar
2 tablespoons fresh
    lemon juice
hot sauce to taste
4 salmon steaks,
    (8 ounces each)

Fresh Pineapple Salsa
1 1/2 cups chopped
    fresh pineapple
1/4 cup chopped red
    onion
2 tablespoons sugar
1 tablespoon fresh
    lemon juice
1/2-1 teaspoon finely
    chopped jalapeno
    pepper to taste
1 teaspoon grated
    fresh ginger
1 tablespoon chopped
    fresh mint

Combine butter, honey, brown sugar, lemon juice and hot sauce in saucepan. Cook over low heat until sugar dissolves and butter melts about 5 minutes. Cool. Marinate salmon steaks for 30 minutes in shallow pan. Oil grill well or use wire fish basket. Cook 4 inches above coals 5 to 7 minutes on one side; turn and cook 5 minutes more. Allow 10 minutes, total, for each 1 inch of thickness of salmon.

To prepare pineapple salsa combine ingredients in bowl. Refrigerate 4 hours. Yields 1 3/4 cups. Garnish each grilled salmon steak with spoonful of salsa.

Serves four.

❦

Salmon Steaks topped with Snapper Mousse

1/2 pound red
   snapper fillets
1 egg
1/4 cup whipping cream
1 teaspoon dried dill or
   3 teaspoons fresh dill
4 6-8 ounce salmon
   steaks-1 inch thick
1 cup dry white wine
4 tablespoons butter

Preheat oven to 450°. To prepare mousse, place snapper in food processor and pulse until broken up. Add the egg, cream and dill, mix well to form mousse.

Arrange salmon steaks in baking dish, cover with white wine, salt and pepper. Evenly spread snapper mousse over each salmon steak. Bake uncovered at 450 for 15 minutes, until mousse is delicately browned. Remove salmon steaks to a plate, cover with foil to keep warm. Pour white wine sauce from baking dish into saucepan. Quickly reduce over high heat to approximately 1/4 cup. Remove from heat and add butter in chunks, whisking constantly until wine sauce thickens slightly. Spoon wine sauce onto plate, then place salmon steak on top. This recipe is easily doubled.

Serves four.

Baked Salmon with Tomato, Cucumber and Basil

John Steinbeck's legendary Cannery Row originated in 1902 when Frank Booth opened Monterey's first factory for packaging sardines. The millions of small, silvery fish that schooled off the Pacific Coast were a golden bonanza for the area. Other canneries soon sprang up along Ocean View Boulevard, former Monterey's Chinatown. During the season, August 1 to February 15, most of Monterey was involved in catching or canning the plentiful sardines. It seemed that the supply of fish was endless as fishermen brought in greater and greater catches each year, making Monterey the largest fishing port on the West Coast. By 1939, there were thirty canneries in operation. That season's catch was 430 million pounds, or approximately 1,290,000,000 sardines. Laid end to end, the fish would have stretched almost to the moon.

Beurre Blanc
3 tablespoons white
 wine vinegar
3 tablespoons dry
 white wine
2 large shallots, minced
1 cup chilled, unsalted
 butter cut into
 16 pieces
1/2 cup diced, peeled,
 seeded plum tomatoes
1/2 cup diced, peeled,
 seeded cucumber

salt and white pepper
3/4 cup loosely packed
 fresh basil, sliced very
 thin into long strips
Salmon
1 3-4 pound salmon
 (1 1/2-1 1/4 inch
 thick) or salmon fillets
salt and white pepper
1 lemon cut into
 very thin circular slices
fresh basil leaves
 for garnish

Preheat oven to 350°. To prepare Beurre Blanc, combine vinegar, wine and shallots into heavy saucepan. Boil until reduced to 1 tablespoon, about 4 minutes. Remove pan from heat and whisk in 2 tablespoons butter. Set pan over low heat and whisk in 1 tablespoon butter 1 piece at a time. If sauce breaks down during process, take off stove and add 2 tablespoons cold butter. If sauce becomes oily or thins after butter is incorporated, it has become too hot. Take 1 tablespoon sauce and mix it with 1 tablespoon cold water in a cold bowl. Mix until creamy. Gradually mix in rest of sauce. Fold in vegetables. Season with salt and pepper.

To prepare salmon place the salmon skin side down. Sprinkle generously with salt and pepper. Bake at 350° until opaque in center, 15 minutes. Arrange lemon slices slightly overlapping across center of salmon. Pour sauce over the top and garnish with basil sprigs.

Serves six to eight.

Seared Salmon Medallions with Ginger Salsa on Tossed Greens

Beat Giger
The Cypress Room, The Lodge at Pebble Beach

8 3-ounce salmon medallions

12 ounces baby greens, washed and dried

Vinaigrette
1 shallot, finely diced
1/4 cup red wine vinegar
1 tablespoon Dijon mustard
1/2 cup extra virgin olive oil

Mix all ingredients and season with salt and pepper.

Scallop Potatoes
8 medium new yellow potatoes, peeled and thinly sliced
1/2 quart cream, season with salt, pepper and 1 chopped clove of garlic

In Pyrex dish layer potatoes and top with seasoned cream. Bake in 375° oven for 45 minutes or until done. Let rest for 45 minutes before preparing dish.

Orange-Ginger Salsa

8 roma tomatoes, peeled and seeded
1 orange, zest and juice
1 tablespoon fresh ginger, diced
1 tableespoon cilantro, diced

Dice tomatoes and put in large mixing bowl. Add ginger, juice and zest of orange, and cilantro. Season with rice vinegar and sesame oil, salt and pepper to taste.

Method of Preparation

Sear salmon in frying pan until done. Toss salad with vinaigrette and divide evenly among 4 plates. Place salmon on top of salad. With a 1 inch round cookie cutter, cut out the scallop potatoes and place evenly around the salad, 4 rounds per plate. Top the salmon with the salsa. Garnish with halved red and yellow cherry tomatoes.

Serves four.

Seared Scallops with Citrus Glaze and Corn Relish

Beat Giger
The Cypress Room, The Lodge at Pebble Beach

20 sea scallops
flour for dredging
   scallops
1/2 cup clarified butter
3/4 cup orange juice
12 tablespoons whole
   butter
8 ounces cooked
   angel hair pasta

Corn Relish
9 ounces kernel corn
3/8 cup diced red and
   green bell peppers
1 green onion, sliced
1/8 cup rice wine vinegar
white pepper to taste
1 1/2 teaspoons sugar

In a 10 inch saute pan heat clarified butter. Dredge scallops in flour and sear in butter until golden brown and cooked. Remove from pan and discard remaining butter. Deglaze pan with orange juice and reduce until juice starts to glaze in pan. Add 4 tablespoons whole butter and stir to mix with orange juice. Put glaze on each scallop on plate.

In a 6 inch saute pan heat 4 tablespoons whole butter. Add all relish ingredients and saute until hot. In another pan heat last 4 tablespoons of whole butter and add cooked pasta, season to taste.

For presentation, alternate a glazed scallop and a spoonful of relish around each serving of pasta.

Serves four.

Orange Roughy with Tomato-Orange Basil Sauce

1 cup fresh orange juice
1/2 cup dry white wine
1/4 cup finely
   minced shallots
2 tablespoons zest
   of orange
4 tablespoon butter
4 fillets orange roughy
6 fresh roma tomatoes,
   seeded and chopped
1/2 cup thinly sliced fresh
   basil leaves
flour for dredging fish
salt and pepper to taste

Combine orange juice, white wine and shallots with half of the orange peel in small, heavy saucepan. Boil until mixture is reduced to 4 tablespoons, about 10 minutes. Set sauce aside. Melt 2 tablespoons butter in pan. Dredge fish in flour; dust off excess. Saute in butter until just cooked through, about 2 minutes per side. Transfer to plate and keep warm. Reheat sauce over low heat. Whisk in remaining 2 tablespoons of butter. Stir in tomatoes, basil and remaining orange zest. Season with salt and pepper to taste. Ladle sauce over fish and serve. Sauce is also good with shellfish or chicken.

Serves four.

Snapper Cortez

The heydeys of Cannery Row were all too short. By 1939 there were warnings of possible depletion of the sardines, but the demand produced by World War II for the canned fish deafened the ears of cannery owners. Although most of Monterey's fishing fleet was requisitioned for coastal patrol, the remaining boats brought in enough sardines to make the 1941-1942 season the most profitable to date. The industry peaked at nearly a quarter million tons processed in 1945.

Decades of overfishing led to an abrupt decline. By 1948, the entire season's catch did not equal a good week earlier in the decade, and by 1950 it was clear the sardines were gone. While many debated the exact cause of the disappearance of the silvery fish, the best answer came from Steinbeck's friend Ed Ricketts: "They disappeared into cans."

3 pounds fresh red
  snapper fillets

Curry Sauce
2 tablespoons butter
2 onions, chopped
2 cups chicken broth
2 tablespoons curry
1/4 teaspoon ginger
1/4 teaspoon tumeric
2 tablespoons flour
3/4 teaspoon salt
1/2 teaspoon pepper
1/4 cup yogurt
1 tablespoon light cream
pinch cayenne and
    paprika

Preheat oven to 375°. Saute onions in butter until soft and opaque, add flour stirring well. Saute 1 minute to lightly cook flour. Add chicken stock, curry, ginger, tumeric, remaining flour, salt and pepper. Cover and simmer 15 minutes. Until slightly thickened. Stir in yogurt, cream, cayenne and paprika.

Pour half of the sauce in a baking dish. Lay the snapper on top of the sauce and pour the remaining sauce over the snapper. Bake at 375° for 30 minutes or until fish is flaky.

Serves eight.

Red Snapper Alvarado

1 1/2 pounds fresh red
    snapper fillets
1/4 cup lime juice
1 yellow onion,
    chopped coarsely
1 green bell pepper,
    chopped coarsely
2 cloves garlic, minced
3 tablespoons
    vegetable oil
1 16-ounce can chopped
    stewed tomatoes
1/3 cup pimento stuffed
    green olives, sliced
1/8 teaspoon crushed hot
    red pepper
1/2 teaspoon cumin
capers for garnish

Place fish in glass dish. Pour lime juice over fish. Set aside. In a large skillet, saute garlic, onion and green bell pepper in vegetable oil until tender. Add sliced olives, tomatoes, red pepper and cumin. Bring to a boil. As the liquid is evaporating, place the snapper fillets on top of the sauce mixture. Cover and simmer until fish is cooked, approximately 4 minutes. Place fish on a plate and spoon sauce over the top. Garnish with capers. Serve with Mexican-style rice and black beans.

Serves four.

Halibut Steaks with Lime Butter in Parchment

Tortilla Flat, Cannery Row and Sweet Thursday are John Steinbeck's trilogy of life in Monterey and along Cannery Row. Tortilla Flat was his fourth book and first success, published in 1935 and written while Steinbeck and his wife Carol lived on 11th street in Pacific Grove. The success of the book prompted Steinbeck to move from the Monterey Peninsula to the hills of Los Gatos. The other two were written in New York, in 1945 and 1954 respectively, but Steinbeck's memories conjure up the smells, the noise, the characters and their trials and the confusion that was life along Cannery Row.

4 6-ounce halibut steaks
    or mahi mahi fillets
1/2 cup butter
1 cup thin sliced
    mushrooms
1/2 cup chopped
    green onion
1 teaspoon zest of lime
4 sheets unwaxed
    parchment

Preheat oven to 350°. Saute all ingredients, except fish. Put one fish portion in middle of each paper. Evenly distribute sauteed mixture over fish. Wrap fish in parchment, making sure it is tightly folded around fish. Bake at 350° for 15 to 20 minutes. Open paper before serving.

Serves four.

Sauteed Halibut With Nectarine Salsa

Salsa
4 ripe nectarines, peeled
    and diced
1/2 red bell pepper, diced
1 cup green onions,
    finely chopped
1/2 cup fresh chives,
    finely chopped
3 teaspoons chopped
    cilantro
juice of two limes

Halibut
3 tablespoons flour
1 1/2 pounds
    halibut fillets
1 ripe nectarine
2 tablespoons peanut oil

To prepare salsa, mix ingredients in a bowl.

To prepare halibut puree remaining nectarine. Cover halibut fillets with puree and marinate for 1 hour. Coat fillets lightly with flour. Heat oil in saucepan and saute fillets, about 3 minutes per side. Arrange on serving plates topped with 4 to 5 tablespoons of the nectarine salsa.

Serves four.

Grilled Swordfish with Mango Chili Relish

2 6-8 ounce
   swordfish steaks
1 tablespoon olive oil
1 ripe mango, diced
   in 1/4 inch cubes
1 jalapeno chili, seeds
   removed, minced
1 tablespoon
   chopped cilantro
1 tablespoon minced
   red onion
1/2 teaspoon
   ground cumin
salt and pepper to taste

Rub the olive oil on the fish, season with salt and pepper. To cut the mango, hold upright on a cutting board, make two cuts along the narrow side of either side of the stem, about 1 inch apart. Take the 2 halves (the flesh of the pit is a perk for the cook) and slice into 4 wedges each. Cut the skin from the fruit and cut into 1/4 inch dices. Combine mango with remaining ingredients. Season to taste and chill.

Grill swordfish about 3 to 4 minutes per side. To serve, arrange fish on plate and spoon relish along one side.

Serves two.

❦

Grilled Swordfish with Szechwan Sauce

4 6 ounce Swordfish
    steaks

Sauce:
2 stalks celery, chopped
1 green bell pepper,
    julienned
1 red bell pepper,

julienned
2 carrots, julienned
2 green onions, chopped
1/2 onion, chopped
1 tablespoon

chopped garlic
2 tablespoons olive oil
1/8 cup lemon juice
1/4 cup white wine
1/4 cup soy sauce
1/2 teaspoon cayenne
    pepper
1/2 teaspoon paprika
3 tomatoes, peeled,
    seeded & diced
1/2 cup sliced
    mushrooms
1/2 teaspoon cornstarch

Saute celery, peppers, carrots, onions and garlic in olive oil until tender. Add lemon juice, wine, soy sauce and spices. Mix. Add mushrooms and tomatoes. Mix. Add cornstarch and stir until thickened.

Smear the swordfish steaks with olive oil and sprinkle with salt and pepper to taste. Place swordfish steaks over medium to hot grill and grill 5 minutes per side. Serve sauce over grilled swordfish.

Serves four.

Swordfish Mar Vista

Central to Steinbeck's books about Cannery Row is Ed Ricketts, a marine biologist and the writer's best friend. Ricketts appears in at least six of Steinbeck's works.

Doc, as he was known locally, moved to Monterey from Chicago without a degree in biology to set up a biological supply house. From his laboratory on Cannery Row he collected marine animal specimens for preparation and shipment to biology classes and educational and medical researchers.

Doc's Pacific Biological Laboratories was also a window on the world of Cannery Row. Across the street was the Lone Star Cafe, the most famous sporting house in town. Down the way, were the Wing Chong Market, owned by Won Yee, and La Ida Cafe, another house of ill repute.

A train wreck ended Rickett's life in 1948 when his aging car stalled on the Del Monte Express tracks at the Drake Avenue crossing.

2 cloves garlic
1 jalapeno pepper, seeded
1 cup chopped celery
(including leaves)
1 medium red onion,
chopped
3 tomatoes, peeled,
seeded and chopped
1/2 bunch chopped
scallions, chopped
4 6-ounce swordfish
fillets (or halibut, mahi
mahi, salmon)
2 tablespoons lime zest

Preheat oven to 350°. To prepare salsa combine first 6 ingredients. Heap on top of fish in baking dish. Top with lime zest. Cover and bake at 350° for 20 minutes. Serves four.

Two Pepper Tuna

4 fillets fresh ahi tuna
3 to 4 peppers sliced in
    1 1/2 x 1/4 inch strips
    use combination of
    red, green and
    yellow peppers
1/4 cup extra virgin
    olive oil
1/2 teaspoon minced
    garlic
juice of 2 lemons
cracked pepper

Combine olive oil, garlic and lemon juice in plastic bag. Add tuna filets. Marinate one hour, turning twice. Remove tuna from marinade. Add pepper strips to marinade. Shake to coat.

Sprinkle cracked pepper, to taste, over both sides of tuna and press in. Heat 1 tablespoon olive oil in frying pan on high. Saute filets for 3 to 4 minutes per side. Remove. Keep warm. Keep pan on high heat and add pepper slices with marinade. Saute peppers 2 to 3 minutes until slightly done. Place tuna on plate. Spoon peppers and any accumulated juices around tuna. Serve with roasted new potatoes, green vegetable and a salad.

Serves four.

Sea Bass with Valley Greens

Per person
1/4 pound Sea Bass fillet
freshly ground
   white pepper to taste
5-6 iceberg lettuce leaves
1 tablespoon balsamic
   vinegar
1 tablespoon olive oil

Thinly slice Sea Bass across grain into four or five thin slices. Season each side with white pepper and salt. Trim lettuce leaves to approximately same size as sea bass slices. Heat a very small skillet over moderate heat until hot and add vinegar and oil. Add lettuce leaves to skillet, turn and transfer to plate as soon as it is wilted. Cook Sea Bass in same manner. Alternate lettuce and sea bass on plate to produce layered entree. Serve immediately.

Serves one.

Mediterranean Casserole

Didier Dutertre
Casanova Restaurant

1 pound halibut	1 cup diced tomato
1 pound rock fish	1/2 cup chopped fennel
16 clams	1 cup diced leeks
16 mussels	1 potato, peeled and
12 prawns	sliced
8 scallops	4 cups fish broth or
4 cloves garlic, crushed	clam juice
1/28 ounce or 1 gram	salt to taste
saffron	1/2 teaspoon cayenne
1 cup extra virgin	1 French baguette, cut
olive oil	into 1/2 inch slices
1 cup chopped onion	

Marinate fish overnight in 1 clove garlic, 1/3 of the saffron, and 1/4 cup olive oil. To prepare broth saute onions in 1/4 cup olive oil. Add 3 cloves of garlic, tomatoes, fennel and leeks. Stir for a few minutes. Add another 1/3 of the saffron, potatoes, and fish broth. Simmer for 15 minutes. Add fish and shellfish except scallops. Simmer 10 minutes adding scallops for the last 3 minutes.

To prepare rouille remove potatoes from broth and place in blender with the remaining garlic, saffron, and olive oil. Add 2 tablespoons broth, a pinch of salt and cayenne pepper. Blend until smooth.

To prepare garlic croutons bread with additional crushed garlic. Place in single layer on baking sheet and bake in 350° oven until lightly toasted. Spread rouille on croutons. Serve fish and broth in large soup bowl with croutons placed around bowl.

Serves 4

This is a version of Bouillabaisse using local fish and shell fish. The original dish calls for specific fish from the mediterranean coast which are unavailable in the Monterey Bay. As a sign of respect for the history of the dish it has been named Mediterranean Casserole.

Casanova Restaurant, located on 5th street between San Carlos and Mission was the tiny home of Aunt Fairybird for over fifty years. Aunt Fairybird had been the cook for Charlie Chaplin and the handy-lady for many Carmel families. Her house was auctioned as part of the estate sale after her death at ninety years old. Walter Georis designed and remodeled Fairybird's house and maintained the warmth and charm of the quaint residence. It is now considered to be "Carmel's most romantic restaurant" by Carmelites as well as world travelers. The Casanova style was born and continues to influence the design of other local buildings.

Flora's Sherried Crab

Make no mistake, this madam was a lady. Flora Woods was a fixture in Cannery Row. The ample woman, normally sporting a red wig and green gown, ran the most famous and most popular sporting house in the area, named The Lone Star in memory of her first husband, a Texas cowboy.

The frivolity of the Lone Star came to an end during World War II when General "Vinegar Joe" Stilwell declared Ocean View Boulevard off limits to Fort Ord soldiers. Shortly afterwards, the Monterey City Council passed an ordinance prohibiting prostitution. Flora and her third husband retired to a second story apartment at the corner of Alvarado and Franklin, where the Wells Fargo building now stands, until her death in 1948 at the age of 72. The town turned out to mourn as she was buried in Monterey's cemetery wearing her favorite red wig.

1/2 pound mushrooms
6 tablespoons butter
3 tablespoons flour
1 cup chicken stock
1/2 cup cream
1 1/2 pounds crab meat,
    picked over
1/2 cup Parmesan cheese
1/2 teaspoon salt
1/8 teaspoon pepper
1/8 teaspoon paprika
3 tablespoons sherry

Saute mushrooms over medium high heat in 3 tablespoons butter, for 3 to 4 minutes. Remove the mushrooms from pan and add the additional 3 tablespoons of butter and the flour. Mix the butter and flour to form a paste. Cook the roux to a blond color without browning. Add the chicken stock and cream and cook over medium to high heat until thickened, 7-10 minutes. Add remaining ingredients, stirring well. Taste for seasoning, more sherry may be added just prior to serving depending on personal taste. Serve in baked puffed shells or over rice. Make the recipe a bit thinner, diluting with chicken stock, if used over rice.

Serves four.

Note: Because of the price of true crab meat, I have used a combination of snapper, shrimp, scallops & a little crab; just as good, although obviously not as rich as using all crab.

Fauna's Lobster Bechamel

1/2 pound mushrooms
2 tablespoons butter
1 tablespoon minced
   onion
1 pound scallops
1 pound fresh lobster,
   picked over
1/2 cup dry vermouth
2 cups Bechamel Sauce
1/2 cup heavy cream

Bechamel Sauce
4 tablespoons butter
4 tablespoons flour
2 cups milk

Cook mushrooms in butter for 5 minutes. Add minced onion and scallops. Continue cooking for 5 minutes. Add lobster and vermouth and cook for ten minutes. Add Bechamel sauce and heavy cream and cook for ten minutes. Serve over rice.

To prepare Bechamel Sauce melt butter over low heat. Add the flour and blend for 3 to 5 minutes. Slowly stir in the milk. Cook and stir the sauce with a wire whisk or wooden spoon until thickened and smooth.

Serves eight to ten.

*F*lora Woods carefully selected both her clientele and her working girls. Her keen financial sense kept businessmen stopping by for drink and discussion. Her girls were trained to be ladies on and off the street and her sense of propriety said "never on Sunday."

She appears in many Steinbeck novels: "Dora Williams" in Tortilla Flat, "Dora Flood" in Cannery Row, "Fauna" in Sweet Thursday, and "Faye" in East of Eden, but her attitude toward her girls is best characterized by "Mack" in Sweet Thursday, "She makes them girls take table-manner lessons and posture lessons." Many of the girls are remembered on the street signs in New Monterey: Lily, Grace, Terry, Alice, Lottie, Jessie.

Flora could always be counted on to give to local community causes and her Christmas list included food given anonymously to as many as 50 families.

Crab Giovanni

2 cups chopped onions
1/2 pound mushrooms,
   sliced
2 cloves garlic, minced
1/2 cup butter, melted
1/2 pound vermicelli,
   cooked
3 cups cooked crab meat,
   picked over
1/2 cup stuffed green
   olives, sliced
1/2 pound cheddar
   cheese, grated
1/2 cup sour cream
1 16-ounce can
   chopped tomatoes
1/2 teaspoon salt
1/2 teaspoon dried basil

Preheat oven to 350°. Saute onions, mushrooms, and garlic in butter until tender. Mix remaining ingredients with onions, garlic and mushrooms and place in greased 9x13 dish and bake uncovered at 350° for 35 to 40 minutes.

Serves eight to ten.

Monterey Bay Etoufee

1/2 cup butter
2 cups chopped
    green onions
3 tablespoons flour
1 1/2 tablespoons paprika
1/2 teaspoon Liquid
    Crab Boil
1 teaspoon creole
    seasoning
1 cup chicken stock
2 tablespoons dry sherry
1 pound crab meat,
    picked over
1 cup cooked artichoke
    hearts, cubed
1/4 cup fresh chopped
    parsley

Melt butter, add 1 1/2 cups green onions, reserving 1/2 cup for garnish, and saute until wilted but not brown. Add flour, stir until bubbly-do not brown. Add seasonings, stock and sherry. Simmer 20 minutes. Add crab meat and artichokes. Simmer 20 additional minutes. Top with remaining 1/2 cup of green onions and parsley before serving over fluffy white rice.

Serves two to four.

The idea for an aquarium along Cannery Row first came in 1914.

In a letter to the city of Monterey, Cannery owner Frank Booth requested permission to build an aquarium between his cannery and Fisherman's Wharf. He offered to cover the costs, estimated at $10,000.

The city fathers turned him down because they thought it would do little to promote tourism or aid the citizens of Monterey.

Crab Cakes with Red Pepper Aioli

Crab Cakes
1 pound Dungeness crab
    meat, picked over
1/4 cup green pepper,
    finely diced
1/4 cup snipped chives
1 cup mashed potatoes
1 egg, lightly beaten
2 teaspoons
    chopped tomato
1 cup fresh breadcrumbs
oil to saute crab cakes

Pepper Aioli
4 red peppers, roasted,
    seeded and peeled
1/2 cup milk
salt and pepper to taste
pinch of cayenne pepper

To prepare crab cakes mix all ingredients except breadcrumbs. Form into six patties and coat with breadcrumbs. Cook crab cakes in oil over medium heat, 4 minutes per side.

To prepare aioli, puree red peppers in food processor until liquid in form. Add 1/2 cup milk to puree. Season. Heat before serving.

Spread individual plates with red pepper aioli; place warm crab cake on top and serve.

Serves two to three.

Crab Cakes with Charon Sauce

Crab Cakes
1 pound diced crab meat, picked over
1 tablespoon diced parsley
1 tablespoon Dijon mustard
1 tablespoon mayonnaise
2 eggs, lightly beaten
1/2 cup fresh breadcrumbs
white pepper
oil for frying

Charon Sauce
3 egg yolks
2 tablespoons lemon juice
1 tablespoon fresh tarragon, or 1/4 teaspoon dried tarragon
pinch of salt and white pepper
3/4 cup butter, melted
1 tablespoon tomato paste

To prepare crab cakes mix all ingredients thoroughly in bowl. Separate evenly into 8 patties. Lightly oil fry pan to prevent sticking. Fry on both sides until lightly browned-transfer to a plate.

To prepare Charon Sauce blend egg yolks in blender on high speed for 10 seconds. Add lemon juice, tarragon and salt and pepper continue to blend. While blender is on high speed add melted butter in a thin stream. To emulsify sauce add tomato paste and blend again.

Top two crab cakes with charon sauce for each person.

Serves four.

Sicilian Marinated Crab

John Pisto
Pisto Restaurants

3 large live crabs	1/4 cup red wine vinegar
6 tablespoons salt	1/2 cup olive oil
4 to 6 garlic cloves	2 teaspoons Dijon
1/2 bunch, handful,	mustard
Italian parsley	pinch crushed red
juice of 1 lemon	pepper flakes

Add salt to 8 quarts of water, bring to a rapid boil. Carefully drop live crabs into pot. Cook for 15 to 20 minutes. While crabs are cooking, prepare the marinating sauce.

Chop garlic cloves coarsely. Remember, the finer the chop, the more powerful the garlic flavor. Chop Italian parsley. Put them in medium mixing bowl and add lemon juice. Whisk in vinegar, olive oil, mustard and crushed red pepper. Salt and pepper to taste.

Remove crabs from pot. Without rinsing, drain and cool until they are cool enough to handle. Remove outer shell and discard. Scrape out remaining crab butter and add to marinating sauce. Remove crab legs. Cut between knuckles for nice serving pieces. Tap each leg gently until cracked. Arrange on large serving platter, and pour the sauce over the crab. Toss gently to coat, and refrigerate for one hour. Serve with crunchy sourdough bread and a green salad.

Serves three.

*Carmel
Mission
Garden*

Mission Roast Pork

*Mission
San Carlos
Borromeo
del Rio
Carmelo*

Carmel-By-The-Sea

Raspberry Souffle

Carmel Beach

Sea Otter in
Monterey Bay

Halibut Steaks with Lime Butter in Parchment

Monterey
Bay Harbor

Monterey Boat Works,
Cannery Row

Zesty Crab & Artichoke Dip

Fisherman's Wharf

Butterfly Shrimp Toast

2 pounds large shrimp, about 30 shrimp

1/3 cup minced bamboo shoots (available canned in Asian food section of market)

1 tablespoon cornstarch

1 tablespoon minced green onion

2 tablespoons dry sherry

2 teaspoons grated ginger root

1 1/2 teaspoons soy sauce

1/8 teaspoon pepper

1 egg

8 thin slices white bread

cilantro sprigs

salad oil

sesame seeds, optional

Shell 16 shrimp, leaving on tails and last shell segments. Butterfly with sharp knife, along the back, split shrimp 3/4 of the way through, stopping at last shell segment. Spread open; rinse under cold water to remove vein. Pat dry; place on plate; cover and refrigerate for two hours. Shell, devein and mince remaining shrimp, until mixture looks like ground meat. In medium bowl, mix minced shrimp and remaining ingredients, except for bread, cilantro and oil.

Cut crusts from bread. Cut each slice into 2 rectangles. Spread two teaspoons of the shrimp mixture evenly on each rectangle. Top each with butterflied shrimp, cut side down, leaving tail extending over narrow end. Evenly spread about 1 tablespoon of mixture over shrimp and bread leaving tail exposed. Gently press cilantro leaf on each slice. Heat 1 inch of salad oil to 325° in large skillet. Carefully place 5 to 6 rectangles, shrimp side down, in oil. Cook until light brown, about 4 minutes. Turn and cook 1 minute more or until bread is golden. Arrange shrimp toast on warm platter, garnish with cilantro. Serve hot. Immediately after frying, shrimp toast may be sprinkled with sesame seed, if desired.

Serves eight.

Confetti Shrimp

1 1/2 pounds uncooked
   large shrimp, shelled
   and deveined
3/4 cup dry white wine or
   dry vermouth
4 tablespoons butter
1 tablespoon chopped
   fresh parsley, basil or
   oregano or a mixture
   of all three
2 to 3 cloves of garlic,
   chopped very fine
1/2 cup chopped sundried
   tomatoes, packed in oil
   & drained
3 to 4 ounces goat
   cheese (plain or herb)
   or feta cheese

Preheat oven to 350°. Layer shrimp in a single layer in large baking dish. Pour the wine or the vermouth over shrimp. Dot shrimp with butter. Sprinkle with herbs, garlic and sundried tomatoes. Crumble the goat cheese over the top. Bake at 350° for 10 minutes or until the shrimp is pink. Remove from the oven and stir to combine cheese throughout. The cheese will not look melted, but when stirred, will melt into a cream sauce. Serve with rice or pasta.

Serves four.

Hot and Sour Prawns with Peanuts and Watercress

24 prawns, peeled
    and devined
1 teaspoon rice wine
    vinegar
2 tablespoons fresh
    grated ginger
2 teaspoons peanut oil
2 tablespoons peanuts
1/2 bunch watercress
1 1/2 cups sliced sweet
    red pepper
1 clove chopped garlic
4 green onions, cut into
    1 inch pieces

Sauce ingredients
1/2 cup chicken stock
2 teaspoons soy sauce
1 1/2 teaspoons
    hoisin sauce
1 teaspoon cornstarch
    dissolved in 1 1/2
    teaspoons rice wine
    vinegar.
1/4 teaspoon sesame oil

Combine shrimp, rice vinegar and grated ginger in large bowl. In small bowl, mix all sauce ingredients well. Heat peanut oil in wok over high heat. Stir fry peanuts for 1 minute. Remove from oil with a slotted spoon, and transfer to a plate. Add watercress to wok, stir fry until wilted, remove from wok. Add peppers and garlic and stir fry for 1 minute. Add shrimp mixture and green onions. Add sauce mixture to wok and cook until clear and thick, stirring often. Spoon sauce and shrimp over watercress, sprinkle with peanuts. Serve with rice.

Serves four.

Many elements of the Monterey Bay Aquarium structure were borrowed from the old Hovden Cannery upon whose foundation the aquarium was built. The pumphouse on the ocean side of the building served Knute Hovden's cannery in earlier years and the building's recurved sea-wall is a cannery-era design that's still effective at dissipating the force of storm waves.

The original boilers downstairs are topped by replicas of cannery smokestacks - an easily recognizable landmark on the Cannery Row horizon.

Five Sauces for Fish

The Monterey Bay Aquarium is visited by 1.7 million people a year drawn by the theatrical display of the ecosystems of the plentiful sealife just under the water.

Aquarium planners made an early decision that the facility would feature only those aquatic plants and animals indigenous to the Monterey Bay.

The result was towering tanks up to three stories tall with glass 7 inches thick recreating life under the sea. Among the favorite exhibits are the 28 foot high kelp forest; a fish eye view of Fisherman's Wharf featuring 30-year-old wharf pilings covered in sea anemones and sea stars, clouds of fish and a 7 gill shark named Emma, the bat ray pool and touch tank where visitors literally get a hands on visit, and the sea otter tank where the playful ocean mammals dive and play, seemingly oblivious of their audience.

For each recipe, pour half the sauce in the baking dish. Lay the fish on top of the sauce and pour the remaining sauce over the fish. Bake at 375 for 30-40 minutes, depending on thickness of fish..

Each recipe is enough to bake a 3 to 4 pounds of fish.

CREOLE SAUCE
1/4 cup oil
1 clove garlic, minced
1 onion, finely chopped
1/2 green pepper, finely chopped
1 tablespoon capers
1 tablespoon chili powder
1 teaspoon salt
1/2 teaspoon allspice
1/4 teaspoon pepper
1/4 teaspoon cloves
10 pitted ripe olives, sliced
3 tomatoes, chopped

Saute the garlic, onions and peppers in the oil. Add the rest of the ingredients and stir well to combine. Try this sauce with red snapper.

CLASSIC SAUCE
6 tablespoons butter
2 tablespoons onion, finely chopped
1 clove garlic, minced
2 tablespoons parsley
1/4 cup dry white wine
juice of one lemon

Saute the onions and garlic in butter until soft and opaque. Add the rest of the ingredients, stirring well to combine. This classic sauce is ideal for sea bass or any firm white fish.

(Continued on next page)

SOUR CREAM SAUCE

5 tablespoons butter
1/4 teaspoon thyme
1 bay leaf, crushed
1 tablespoon onion, finely
   chopped
3/4 teaspoon dill or
   1 tablespoon fresh dill
1/4 teaspoon salt
1/4 teaspoon fresh
   ground pepper
1 cup sour cream
1/4 cup light cream

Melt the butter and add all ingredients. Mix well. Sour cream sauce is particularly good with halibut.

HERB SAUCE

6 tablespoons butter,
   melted
2 onions, chopped
2 stalks celery, chopped
1 cup mushrooms, sliced
2 tablespoons fresh
   parsley, chopped
1/4 teaspoon thyme
1/4 teaspoon tarragon
1/4 teaspoon rosemary

Melt butter in skillet. Saute onions and celery until opaque and soft. Add mushrooms and saute 2 minutes. Add herbs. Serve this herb sauce with sole.

SPINACH PESTO SAUCE

1 cup packed, fresh
   spinach leaves, washed
   & stemmed
2 tablespoons pine nuts
4 cloves garlic
1 cup grated Parmesan
   cheese
1/2 cup olive oil

Combine all ingredients in a food processor or blender, and blend into a smooth sauce. Spinach Pesto Sauce is wonderful on salmon steaks.

It takes a lot of volunteers to keep the aquarium open. The facility relies on a volunteer corps of 550 participants to support all aspects of the operation. Roughly, 350 volunteers are aquarium guides, with at least 45 hours of training, who help interpret the many exhibits for visitors. Another 70 people volunteer as divers to aid in aquarium operations. Others offer their services in the office, bookstore and information desk. In total, more than 65,000 hours annually are donated by the group of local volunteers.

Avocado Stuffed with Seviche

1 pound scallops
3/4 cup lemon juice
1/4 cup lime juice
3 tomatoes, peeled,
   seeded and diced
1 serrano or jalapeno
   chili, seeded and
   minced
1/3 cup salad oil
2 tablespoons dry
   white wine

1 teaspoon fresh thyme
1 teaspoon fresh chervil
   or parsley
1 tablespoon chopped
   fresh cilantro
1/2 teaspoon black
   pepper
3 avocados
1 medium red onion,
   thinly sliced

Rinse scallops and pat dry. If they are large, cut into 3/4 inch cubes. Place scallops in large bowl and cover with lemon and lime juice. Cool at room temperature 3 hours, turning occasionally with wooden spoon. Add tomatoes, chilies, oil, wine and seasonings. Toss well and refrigerate, covered, 4 hours or overnight.

To serve: Peel avocados and slice in half lengthwise, remove pits. Drain scallops and spoon into avocados. Arrange sliced onions on top. Can also be served in 'salade compose' style - arrange butter leaves on individual plates, make spiral with avocado slices. Arrange scallops on top of avocados, sprinkling marinade over greens. Garnish with onion.

Serves six.

MEATS & POULTRY

Monterey

It was the capital of Spanish California, where traders registered at the Custom House to do business in tallow and hides with the local rancheros. In the bay, Commodore Sloat sailed to a bloodless victory, capturing California for the United States. And here, the leaders of the new American territory came to draft the state's first constitution.

For more than 200 years Monterey has reigned as the queen city on California's coast. Original adobes that housed prominent families, the state's first theater, and profitable whaling businesses now serve as art museums, community rooms, and bank headquarters. The structures of the future build on the designs of the past and ordinary becomes extraordinary.

Individual Beef Wellington

Beef Wellington
1 3-pound beef tender-
   loin, trimmed and
   cut into 6 equal pieces
   or 6 8-ounce fillet
   mignons, trimmed of
   fat

2 tablespoons oil
1 package (17 1/4
   ounces) frozen puff
   pastry sheets, thawed
1/2 cup fresh or canned
   pate de foie gras
1 egg, lightly beaten

Preheat oven to 425°. Quickly sear meat on both sides in the oil over high heat. Remove from pan and cool to room temperature. Roll out pastry sheet to 14x14 inch square. Cut pastry into 4 equal portions. Repeat with second sheet. Spread each cooled fillet with 1 generous tablespoon of pate. Place each fillet, pate side down onto pastry square. Wrap each pastry envelope style by gathering opposite corners. Place Wellingtons seam side down on a greased baking sheet. Pinch ends firmly. Cut steam vents on top. Decorate with pastry cutouts made from remaining 2 squares. Brush pastry with beaten egg to ensure brown crust. Bake 10 minutes at 425°. Reduce heat to 350° and bake 5 to 8 more minutes or until pastry is golden brown and puffed. Wellingtons can be prepared 4 hours ahead of time and refrigerated.

Madeira Sauce:
Reduce 1 cup of your favorite brown sauce to 3/4 cup. Add 1/4 cup dry madeira. Cover and simmer on medium low heat for 15 minutes. Swirl in 1 tablespoon of butter and 2 more tablespoons of madeira.

To serve, spoon 2 to 3 tablespoons of hot madeira sauce on plate. Top with a Wellington. Pastry under Wellington will be a little soggy - this will help camouflage and make a nice presentation.

Serves six.

As a substitute for the pate de foie gras make mushrooms duxelles

1/2 pound mushrooms,
   very finely chopped
1/4 cup finely chopped onion
   or 2 tablespoons finely
   chopped shallots
2 tablespoons butter
1 tablespoon oil
salt and pepper to taste

Saute chopped onion in butter/oil mixture over medium heat until golden. Add mushrooms and increase heat to high. Quickly saute until mushrooms have rendered their juices and they have been evaporated. Remove from heat and season to taste. Mixture should be dry and highly seasoned. Cool well before using.

Grilled Steak Fromaggio

S *panish settlement in Monterey took a two-pronged approach. The military established a presidio, or military base, to house soldiers necessary to claim the land for Spain. They were accompanied by friars or priests ready to claim the souls of the local inhabitants for the Catholic church.*

Construction of the first Presidio and mission in Monterey began in a rectangular plot, bordered by present day Fremont, Abrego, Webster, and Estero Streets.

4 8-ounce New York
   strip steaks, 1 inch
   thick, butterflied by
   cutting almost in
   half lengthwise
1 cup grated
   mozzarella cheese
16 sun dried tomatoes,
   packed in oil, drained
4 tablespoons toasted
   pine nuts
8 slices of pancetta
2 bunches fresh spinach,
   washed well and
   stemmed
2 tablespoons olive oil

Sear steaks on hot grill 2 to 3 minutes on each side until brown. Remove steaks from grill and stuff each with 1/4 cup mozzarella, 4 sun dried tomatoes, and 1 tablespoon toasted pine nuts. Close steaks and wrap each with 2 pieces of pancetta. Return to grill and cook until tender or until desired doneness.

Place cleaned spinach in 2 tablespoons hot olive oil in a frying pan. Cook until tender, 2 to 3 minutes. Remove from pan and drain.

Place a small bed of spinach on each plate. Slice each steak diagonally in thin slices and present fanned on top of a bed of spinach.

Serves four.

Bistro Steak

1 3/4 cups beef stock
8 tablespoons butter
1 tablespoon oil
4 8-ounce New York
   strip steaks, 1 inch
   thick, salt and
   peppered to taste
4 shallots, finely chopped
1 tablespoon finely
   chopped fresh thyme
2/3 cup dry red wine

Boil stock in small saucepan until reduced by half. Set aside. Melt 2 tablespoon butter and oil over medium high heat in a large skillet. Add the seasoned steaks and cook steaks 3 minutes per side for rare or until desired doneness. Remove to platter and cover with foil. Saute shallots and thyme until soft. Add wine and reduce by half. Add broth and reduce by half again. Reduce heat and whisk in remaining 6 tablespoons of butter, 1 tablespoon at a time. Return steaks to pan and coat with sauce.

Serves four.

Spicy Grilled London Broil

In 1818, the city of Monterey was captured and burned by the famed French pirate Hippolyte de Bouchard.

Serving in the patriot navy of the revolutionary "Republic of Buenos Aries," Bouchard attacked Monterey as the seat of Spanish authority and power in Alta California. After requesting the townspeople to surrender, Bouchard landed several hundred men with weapons on the beach. Monterey residents beat a hasty retreat and the invaders looted and sacked the town, then set it afire. Hippolyte de Bouchard and his followers left Monterey with its treasures and never returned.

1 1/4 pounds London
   broil

Marinade
3/4 cup olive oil
1/4 cup wine vinegar
1/4 cup red wine
1 teaspoon minced garlic
2 green onions, chopped
1 teaspoon thyme
1 teaspoon rosemary
1/2 teaspoon salt
1 tablespoon coarsely
   ground black pepper

Mix marinade ingredients together and pour over meat. Marinate overnight, turning meat several times. Grill meat to desired doneness, approximately 6 to 10 minutes per side. Slice meat diagonally across grain in thin slices.

Serves four to six.

Spanish Kabobs

1 pound sirloin steak,
   cubed
1 large onion, cut in
   chunks
1 green bell pepper, cut
   in chunks
1 jicama, cut in chunks
6 large mushrooms,
   cut in half

Marinade
1 cup red wine
1/3 cup olive oil
1 jalepeno pepper,
   finely chopped
1/2 teaspoon ground
   cumin
1 clove garlic, minced

Arrange meat and vegetables on skewers. Mix marinade in shallow pan and marinate kabobs 2-4 hours.

Barbecue kabobs 4 to 5 minutes over hot coals. Serve over seasoned mexican style rice.

Serves six to eight.

Belgian Beef Stew

1/4 pound lean bacon, diced
1 tablespoon butter
20 small white onions, peeled
1 clove garlic, minced
2 pounds boneless chuck or round roast, cut into 1 1/2 inch cubes
2 tablespoons flour
2 teaspoons salt
1/4 teaspoon fresh ground pepper
12 ounces dark beer
1 tablespoon lemon juice

Pour boiling water over bacon and let stand for 1 minute, drain. Put bacon and butter into a large skillet. Cook until the bacon is limp and transparent. Add onions and garlic; cook, stirring frequently until golden. Transfer bacon and onions to dutch oven or flameproof casserole. Add beef to the fat in the skillet, a few pieces at a time, and brown over high heat. Transfer meat to the casserole. Stir in flour, salt, and pepper. Add beer to barely cover meat. Bring to boiling. Reduce heat and simmer, covered for 1 1/2 hours or until meat is tender. Check for moisture and, if necessary, add more beer. Taste for seasonings ; add more salt, or pepper to taste. Remove dutch oven from heat and stir in lemon juice. Serve with noodles and garnish with chopped parsley.

Serves six to eight.

Bobotie

3 tablespoons oil
1/2 pound ground beef
1/2 pound ground lamb
1 3/4 cups chopped onion
2 tablespoons curry
  powder
4 large cloves garlic,
  chopped
3/4 cup raisins
2/3 cup strained
  lemon juice
1/2 cup apricot preserves

1/2 cup chopped
  dried apricots
2 teaspoons minced hot
  pepper or chili flakes
1/2 teaspoon salt
2/3 cup half and half
1/2 cup dry, fine white
  bread crumbs

Topping
4 eggs
2 cups milk

Heat oil in large skillet over medium to medium high heat. Add ground meats and cook until no longer pink, about 5 minutes. Add onions and stir until slightly brown. Add curry and garlic. Stir 2 minutes. Add raisins, lemon juice, preserves, apricots, hot pepper and salt. Stir until mixture thickens and most of lemon juice evaporates, about 5 minutes. Mix in half and half and bread crumbs. Pour into a 7x12 baking pan and cool completely. If desired, can be prepared a day ahead to this point. Refrigerate tightly covered. To complete preparation bring back to room temperature before finishing. Preheat oven to 350°. To prepare topping whisk milk with eggs, season with salt and pour over meat mixture. Bake 35 to 45 minutes or until topping is set. Serve with wild rice or the grain of your choice. Makes a great buffet dish.

Serves eight.

Lamb Stew with Cumin Seed Pasta

As the capital, Monterey was designated as the port of entry for all goods being sold in Alta California. Any merchants wanting to do business in Mexican California had to first come to Monterey to register at the Customs House. This made Monterey the business center as well as the political center of California. It also brought a large number of Americans to Monterey.

3 1/2 pounds lamb stew
   meat, cut in 1 to 1 1/2
   inch cubes
1 cup flour
3 teaspoons salt
1 teaspoon pepper
4 tablespoons olive oil
1 onion, finely chopped
4 cloves garlic,
   finely minced
1 teaspoon rosemary

1/2 teaspoon thyme
1/2 teaspoon sugar
1 cup dry white wine
1 cup beef stock
1 14 ounce can chopped
   plum tomatoes,
   drained
1 tablespoon cumin seeds
1 pound penne pasta
4 tablespoons butter

Dredge lamb in flour seasoned with 2 teaspoons of the salt and the pepper. Brown lamb cubes in olive oil. Add onions and garlic and continue to brown another few minutes. Add rosemary, thyme, 1 teaspoon salt, sugar, wine and stock. Simmer slowly until tender, about 1 1/2 hours. Add tomatoes for the final 20 minutes of cooking.

Toast the cumin seed in a skillet for 3 to 4 minutes or until fragrant and slightly darkened. Cook pasta in boiling water for 6 to 8 minutes. Drain, and add butter and toasted seeds. Toss together, salt and pepper to taste. Serve lamb stew over prepared pasta.

Serves eight.

Pesto Lamb d'Elegance

1 5 to 6 pound leg
  of lamb
1 cup pesto sauce
1 cup shallots, peeled
  and sliced
2 medium heads
  radicchio, cut into 4
  wedges each
fresh basil sprigs

Cut excess fat from leg of lamb, leaving a thin layer. Set lamb on rack in roasting pan. Make 10 to 12 slits in lamb and spoon some pesto sauce into each slit. Cover lamb and let stand for 2 hours at room temperature or refrigerate overnight. Preheat oven to 350°. Roast lamb 30 minutes. Add shallots to pan, turning to coat in pan juices. Roast 45 minutes. Add radicchio, turning to coat in juices. Continue to roast until thermometer inserted into thickest part of meat registers 140° for medium rare. (Approximately 45 minutes) Remove from oven and let stand for 15 minutes. Transfer to platter, garnish with fresh basil sprigs and serve.

If radicchio is unavailable 4 heads of Belgian endive cut in half lengthwise may be substituted.

Serves eight.

Basil Pesto Sauce

1 cup fresh basil leaves
4 spinach leaves
6 sprigs parsley
3 sprigs marjoram
1/3 cup pine nuts
3 cloves garlic, crushed
1/3 cup grated
  Parmesan cheese
1/3 cup grated Romano cheese
3 tablespoons olive oil
2 tablespoons butter
1/4 teaspoon salt

Mix all ingredients in the blender until well mixed and smooth.

Leg of Lamb with Apricot Sauce

1 6-pound leg of lamb,
   trimmed of most fat
   but leaving the fell,
   the parchment like
   skin, intact
4 to 6 good size cloves
   of garlic.

Sauce
2 large yellow onions,
   chopped fine
2 tablespoons butter
1/2 large garlic clove
2 cups apricot jam
1 teaspoon salt
dash cayenne pepper
3 tablespoons cider
   vinegar
1/4 cup brown sugar

To prepare lamb, cut garlic cloves into halves or quarters. Stud lamb with garlic by making slits in the meat with a sharp knife and inserting the cloves.

Preheat oven to 450°. Place studded lamb fat side up on a rack in baking pan. Place in oven, immediately reducing heat to 325°. Roast 2 1/2 hours, approximately 25 minutes per pound or until internal temperature reaches 160° - 165° for medium rare to 175° - 180° for well done meat. 20 minutes before lamb is done pull from oven and remove fell from lamb and discard. Return to oven and baste with sauce while lamb completes cooking.

To prepare sauce, saute onions in the butter until golden brown. Add the remaining ingredients and simmer gently for 1 hour, stirring occasionally. If sauce becomes too thick, thin with a little water. After basting, serve remaining sauce at the table. Green peas and oven-fried potatoes are good accompaniments with a light tossed green salad.

Serves eight.

El Estero Lamb Stew

3 pounds lamb, cut into 1 to 1 1/2 inch cubes

flour to coat lamb

4 tablespoons cooking oil

6 juniper berries, crushed

1/4 teaspoon fresh ground black pepper

2 cloves garlic, crushed

2 yellow onions, peeled and chopped

1 medium dried red chili, crushed or 1/2 teaspoon red chili flakes

1/2 cup chopped parsley

6 whole canned green chili peppers, diced

1 quart water

2 teaspoons dried oregano

1 tablespoon salt

5 1/2 cups canned white pearl hominy with liquid

Dredge lamb in flour. Heat oil in heavy pot over medium to medium high heat. Add lamb cubes and cook until brown. Stir in black pepper and juniper berries. Occasionally stir until meat is thoroughly browned. Remove meat from pot. Add onions and saute until golden. Add garlic. Return meat and add remaining ingredients plus 1 quart water. Cover. Simmer 1 1/2 hours, stirring occasionally. Serve with green salad and flour tortillas or sweet bread. Leftover leg of lamb works great in this recipe. Freezes well.

Serves twelve.

Pork Medallions with Dijon Sauce

The Monterey Custom House is the only building still standing in California that was built to take care of important government functions. It was more than a place for the collection of tariffs; it was a gathering place for the community. Ships brought news as well as merchandise from all over the world. The official papers of the Mexican government signed by the governor were stamped "Aduana Maritima, Monterey," indicating that the Custom House served as a capitol. Social gatherings of the Californios were held there. And it was here that Commodore Thomas Sloat raised the American flag on California soil.

1 pound pork tenderloin
1/3 cup flour
1/2 teaspoon pepper
3 tablespoons butter
5 green onions, chopped
1/2 cup dry white wine
1 cup whipping cream
1/3 cup Dijon mustard

Cut tenderloin crosswise into 1/2 inch thick pieces. Pound between sheets of waxed paper to thickness of 1/4 inch. Combine flour and pepper in shallow dish. Melt 1 tablespoon butter in heavy skillet over medium high heat. Dredge pork in flour, shake off excess. Add 1/3 of pork to skillet and saute until brown and cooked through, about 2 minutes per side. Transfer to platter and keep warm. Repeat with remaining pork in 2 batches. Add 1 tablespoon butter for each batch. Add green onions to skillet and saute just until tender, about 1 minute. Stir in white wine and boil until liquid is reduced to 2 tablespoons, about 3 minutes. Add whipping cream and simmer until thickened. Whisk in Dijon mustard. Spoon sauce over pork and serve. Garnish with additional green onions.

Serves four.

Delectable Pork Roast

2 or 3 small pork
   tenderloins
2 tablespoons dry
   mustard
2 teaspoons leaf thyme
1/2 cup dry sherry
1/2 cup soy sauce
2 cloves
1 large clove garlic,
   minced
1 teaspoon dried ginger

Sauce
1 10-ounce jar
   currant jelly
1 tablespoon soy sauce
2 tablespoons sherry

Place tenderloins in shallow pan. Rub with mixture of mustard and thyme. Combine sherry, soy sauce, cloves, garlic powder and ginger. Pour over meat. Let stand 3 to 4 hours at room temperature or overnight covered in refrigerator. Turn the meat over frequently. Pour off marinade when ready to cook, reserving some. Roast uncovered at 325° for 1 hour, baste with marinade. As an alternative to roasting, you can barbecue the pork. The taste is altogether different and just as delicious. Slice pork into medallions and serve with sauce.

Sauce: Over medium heat melt the jelly, add soy sauce, and sherry. Stir and simmer for 2 minutes.

Serves six to eight.

"Our cargo was an assorted one: that is, it consisted of everything under the sun. We had spirits of all kinds (sold by the cask), teas, coffee, sugar, spices, raisins, molasses, hardware, crockery-ware, tin-ware, cutlery, clothing of all kinds, boots and shoes from Lynn, calicoes and cottons from Lowell, crapes, silks, also shawls, scarfs, necklaces, jewelry, and combs for women; furniture, and in fact everything that can be imagined, from Chinese fireworks to English cartwheels..."

– Richard Henry Dana
Two Years Before the Mast

Crown Roast of Pork

1 crown roast of pork made from 2 center-cut pork loins 8-9 pounds. Have butcher prepare and save you the ground trimmings.
Salt and pepper
1 cup dried figs, chopped
1 cup dried peaches, chopped
1 cup dried apricots, chopped
1 cup pitted prunes, chopped
1 cup dried pears, chopped
1 cup currants
1 cup apples, cored and chopped
1 cup dates, chopped
1 large onion, minced
1 lemon, thinly sliced and seeded
2 cups finely crushed biscotti crumbs
1 cup white port

Preheat oven 350°. Salt and pepper pork and stand it in a foil-lined shallow roasting pan.

To prepare stuffing, brown the pork ground trimmings found in the center of roast in a large skillet, over medium heat. Drain fat. Add all remaining ingredients and stir in wine. Stuff the center of the roast. Cover the stuffing with foil. Roast for 2 1/2 to 3 hours , or 180° on meat thermometer.

Substitute fruits if desired. Garnish roast with brandied fruits, herbs, or crab apples. Stuffing can be prepared 1 day in advance.

Serves eight to ten.

Spiced Pork Tenderloin

4 pork tenderloins,
   trimmed
4 cloves garlic
1 1/2 inch fresh
   ginger root
4 tablespoons soy sauce
1/4 cup dark rum
1/2 jalepeno pepper,
   seeded and chopped
5 tablespoons
   hoisin sauce

Put all ingredients, except pork, in blender or food processor and process until chopped. Put pork in plastic bag with marinade, seal out air and marinate 4 hours or overnight.

Preheat oven to 350°, wrap pork in foil with marinade and bake at 350° to an internal temperature of 140°, approximately 30 to 35 minutes a pound.

For barbecue, grill until brown on outside and pink inside, about 20 to 25 minutes.

Slice on the diagonal to serve.

Serves eight.

*M*onterey was ruled by the upper class caste, an oligarchy of families, most claiming pure Spanish ancestry, striving to speak purest Castilian and intermarrying to keep their bloodlines pure. Alvarado, Vallejo, Castro, Munras, Estradas and the Soberanes all were important families politically as well as socially in the Californian capital.

Pork Tenderloin Normande

Cranberry Chutney

1 pound cranberries

1 cup golden
seedless raisins

1 2/3 cups sugar

1 tablespoon cinnamon

1 1/2 teaspoons
ground ginger

1/4 teaspoon whole cloves

1 cup dry white wine
or water

1/2 cup chopped onion

1 apple, peeled and
chopped

1/2 cup chopped celery

Combine cranberries, raisins, sugar, spices and wine or water. Cook about 15 minutes, until thickened. Stir in everything else and simmer another 15 to 20 minutes. Cool and refrigerate. If you don't like raisins, exclude and add an extra apple.

This is a delightful alternative to ordinary cranberry dishes at holiday time. Serve with turkey, pork or chicken. Serves twelve.

1 tablespoon oil
1 tablespoon butter
2 pork tenderloins,
1 1/2 pounds total
2 medium onions, diced
2 tart apples, peeled,
cored and sliced
3 tablespoons Calvados
1 tablespoon flour
1 1/2 cups chicken
or veal stock

salt & pepper
1/3 cup heavy cream
or creme fraiche

For the garnish
2 tablespoons butter
2 firm apples, unpeeled,
but sliced
2 tablespoons sugar
1 bunch watercress

In a saute pan or shallow casserole, heat the oil and butter and brown the tenderloins on all sides. Remove them, add the onion and cook until soft. Add the apple slices and cook over medium high heat until apples and onions are golden brown. Replace the tenderloins. Add the Calvados and flame. Stir the flour into the pan juices. Add the stock and bring to a boil. Cover, simmer until meat is tender, 40-50 minutes, stirring occasionally.

To prepare the garnish, melt butter in a frying pan. Dip each side of apple slice in sugar. Cook over medium high heat until sugar is caramelized, turning over after 4 to 5 minutes.

To assemble, lift the tenderloin out of the pan. Carve into 1/4 inch slices on diagonal. Keep warm. Strain the sauce, pressing down to puree apples. Add the cream and bring to boil, and reduce to coating consistency. Taste for seasonings. Spoon sauce over pork and garnish with caramelized apples and watercress. It's good with rice pilaf.

Serves four.

Mission Roast Pork

4 to 5 pound loin of
  pork roast
1/4 cup of olive oil
1/2 green pepper,
  chopped
1 onion, chopped
1 clove garlic, crushed
1 teaspoon salt
1/2 teaspoon pepper
2 cups tomato sauce
1 3/4 cups chicken or
  beef stock
1/4 cup sherry
1 1/2 tablespoons chili
  powder
1/2 cup raisins
1 cup stuffed green
  olives, chopped
2 cups cooked rice

Cut a large pocket in the roast at end of ribs for stuffing.
Set aside. Saute green pepper, onion, and garlic in olive
oil over medium high heat until tender. Add salt and
pepper, tomato sauce and stock. Let simmer. Add sherry
and chili powder. Continue to simmer. Add chopped
olives and raisins and simmer five minutes more. Add
3/4 cup of sauce to rice and stuff roast. Roast at 350° for
two hours. At the end of the first hour take off excess fat,
spoon extra sauce and rice over and around roast. Return
to oven for final hour. Stuffing can be made a day in
advance.

Serves six.

*T*he American flag was
finally raised, for good,
over California on July 7,
1846, by Commodore Thomas
Sloat after he bloodlessly
captured Monterey, and
California, for the United
States. In typical fashion,
the residents of Monterey
responded by throwing a
fiesta in honor of the event.

Veal Tallyrand

1 1/2 pound veal
   scallopini
3 tablespoons butter
1/2 cup heavy cream
6 large mushrooms,
   finely chopped
2 tablespoons finely
   chopped shallots
1 1/2 tablespoons
   lemon juice
1 teaspoon finely
   chopped parsley
2 egg yolks
Salt and white pepper
   to taste

In a skillet, lightly brown veal in 3 tablespoons of butter over medium heat. Remove veal from skillet. Add to drippings mushrooms and shallots to drippings, and cook until limp but not brown. Return veal to skillet and add cream. Simmer for 8 to 10 minutes. In small bowl, mix lemon juice, parsley and 2 egg yolks, until slightly beaten. Add 3 tablespoons of cream sauce into the egg mixture slowly being careful not to cook the eggs. Pour egg mixture into remaining cream sauce. Season with salt and white pepper.

Serves six.

Veal Marengo

1 1/2 to 2 pounds
 boneless rump or
 shoulder of veal, cut
 into 1-1 1/2 inch
 cubes
2 tablespoons oil
1 onion, sliced
1 tablespoon flour
1/2 cup white wine
1 1/2 to 2 cups veal
 or beef stock
1 tablespoon fresh thyme

2 cloves garlic, crushed
1 bay leaf
3 tomatoes, peeled,
 seeded and coarsely
 chopped (or 1 pound
 can chopped plum
 tomatoes, drained)
salt and pepper to taste
1/3 pound mushrooms,
 quartered
parsley , chopped

In a heavy saute pan or casserole, heat the oil over medium to medium high heat and brown the veal, a few pieces at a time. Remove the veal, add the onions and cook until soft. Add the flour and cook, stirring until onions and flour are well browned. Stir in 1 cup of the stock, the wine, thyme, bay leaf, garlic and tomatoes. Replace the veal and bring to a boil. Cover the pan 3/4 of the way with a lid and cook in oven 1 1/4 to 1 1/2 hours, or until tender. Add mushrooms during last 1/2 hour of cooking. The cooking liquid should evaporate to about 1 cup while cooking. If it reduces more, add the remaining 1/2 cup of stock. Taste for salt and pepper. Remove bay leaf. Sprinkle with chopped parsley. May be served with rice or noodles. This dish can be prepared up to 3 days in advance and kept covered in the refrigerator.

Serves six.

The first American alcalde - or mayor - of Monterey left a permanent mark on the city. A chaplain in Sloat's fleet, Walter Colton was a former professor and newspaper editor. During his three year administration, he constructed the first town hall. The two story building was built at practically no cost to the city using prison labor and was financed by the sale of town lots, fines on gamblers, and taxes on liquor stores.

Veal with Tomato, Caper and Pine Nut Sauce

4 11-ounce veal rib
   chops, boned and
   trimmed of fat
2 tablespoons olive oil
4 ripe tomatoes, peeled,
   seeded and chopped
1/3 cup pine nuts, toasted
2 tablespoons capers,
   drained
1 tablespoon
   chopped shallot
1 tablespoon chopped
   fresh garlic

1 tablespoon minced
   fresh basil or
   1 teaspoon dried
1 teaspoon minced fresh
   oregano or 1/4
   teaspoon dried
4 tablespoons dry
   white wine
1 tablespoon fresh
   lemon juice
2 tablespoons butter

Season veal with salt and pepper. Heat 1 tablespoon olive oil in skillet. Add veal and brown on both sides. Cook veal about 10 minutes for medium rare. Transfer veal to platter and cover with aluminum foil to keep warm. Add remaining tablespoon olive oil to same skillet, set over medium heat. Add tomatoes, pine nuts, capers, shallots, garlic, all herbs and saute 2 minutes. Add wine, lemon juice and simmer about 4 minutes. Whisk in butter. Pour over veal. Garnish with pine nuts.

Serves four.

Veal Rolls Del Monte

6 slices of veal scaloppine
1/4 pound prosciutto
1/2 cup fresh cooked
    spinach, squeezed dry
    and chopped
6 tablespoons
    Parmesan cheese
3 tablespoons
    vegetable oil
1/2 cup dry white wine
3 tablespoons
    tomato paste
Freshly ground
    black pepper

Pound the veal and trim to approximately 6x4 inches. Reserve the trimmings. In a food processor with the steel blade, combine the prosciutto, spinach, Parmesan cheese, and the veal trimmings. Process to blend. Divide into six servings and place in the center of each piece of veal. Roll the veal into tight compact rolls and secure with one or two toothpicks. In a heavy skillet, heat the vegetable oil and add the veal rolls and brown on all sides. Reduce the heat and cook for approximately 10 minutes. Be careful not to overcook. Remove the rolls and increase the heat. Deglaze the skillet with the white wine. Reduce heat and add the tomato paste. Add more wine or water if needed to make a medium thick sauce. Remove the toothpicks and return the rolls to the skillet and heat through. May be made ahead and refrigerated. To serve, bring to room temperature and heat in a 325° oven for 10 minutes.

Serve four to six.

There were 48 delegates to the California Constitutional Convention September 1, 1849. Ten were from the southern part of the state the rest from the northern end, reflecting the demographics of the state at the time. San Francisco and Sacramento led the field with eight delegates each; San Jose had seven; San Joaquin and Monterey, six each; Los Angeles, five; Sonoma, three; San Diego and San Luis Obispo, two each; and Santa Barbara had only one.

Chicken Junipero

1 broiler chicken (about 4
   pounds) cut in pieces,
   skin removed
1/2 cup dry sherry
1/2 cup honey
1/2 cup flour
8 tablespoons butter
1 1/2 cups gin
1/2 cup chopped parsley
1/2 cup chopped onion
1/2 teaspoon dried
   tarragon
2 teaspoons arrowroot
1 cup cream
salt
sesame seeds

Preheat oven to 350°. Mix together sherry and honey,
stirring well to combine. Rub chicken with sherry/honey
sauce. Dust lightly with flour and brown in butter.
Arrange in buttered baking dish, pour gin over chicken
and sprinkle with parsley, onion and tarragon. Bake in
350° oven for 1 hour. Remove chicken, keeping warm.

To make sauce, pour accumulated juices from baking
dish into saucepan or original skillet, reserving 1/2 cup.
Mix the 1/2 cup reserved juices with the arrowroot and
add to the pan along with the cream and cook over
medium high heat until thickened. Salt to taste. Spoon
sauce over chicken. Sprinkle with sesame seeds.

Serves four to six.

Basted Chicken with Plum Sauce

4 chicken breasts (or one
    whole chicken, cut up)
1 teaspoon garlic salt
1 teaspoon black pepper

Plum Sauce
1 8 ounce jar plum jelly
1/2 cup chopped
    green onions
1 teaspoon Chinese
    5 spice mixture
1/3 cup red wine vinegar
1 tablespoon soy sauce
1 tablespoon ground
    ginger

Preheat oven to 450°. Place chicken, bone side down, in glass pan. Sprinkle with garlic salt and pepper. Bake, uncovered, for 20 minutes at 450°. Pour off accumulated fat and liquid from pan and discard. Make plum sauce by melting plum jelly in saucepan over medium heat. Add remaining ingredients and stir to combine. Turn chicken over and pour plum sauce on top. Cook about 40 minutes at 350°, basting and turning several times. Serve with rice. Pour some sauce over meat to serve; pass additional sauce.

Serves four.

❧

Walter Colton and Robert Semple established California's first newspaper, *The Californian*. Semple, a true mountain man who served as president of the California Constitutional Convention, stood six feet eight inches in his buckskins. He was as quick with his pen as he was with his rifle, however.

This odd couple found an old press used in Mission days, cleaned off the typeface, improvised with tin instead of lead, and put together a usable press. The publication was printed weekly on cigarette paper.

There were, however, no "W's" in the type, so Colton and Semple put together two "V's" for use in their paper.

❧

Laab Gai

Wanda and Pierre Coutou combine the best of their culinary cultures in more than 50 specialties of Thai and French influence at their restaurant in Carmel Valley. The name Thai Bistro illustrates this charming combination perfectly; Thai indicates the authentic recipes from Wanda's country and Bistro suggests the classic French deserts that Pierre's influence brings to the menu.

Thai Bistro received the Best Restaurant Award from Adventures in Dining magazine in 1993. The restaurant was also given the distinction of catering "High Tea" at Stanford University in honor of the Queen of Thailand, Queen Sirikit, during her visit to California.

Boneless chicken in lime juice, shallots, mint and chili

Wanda Coutou
Thai Bistro

1 breast of chicken, skinned and boned	4 or 5 fresh mint leaves, torn into pieces
2 shallots, sliced	1/2 teaspoon dry chili pepper
1 lime or lemon, juiced	3 teaspoons ground roasted rice
1 green onion, finely sliced	1 small cabbage, quartered
1 teaspoon Oriental fish sauce	lettuce, tomatoes, and cucumber for garnish
1 teaspoon oyster sauce	

To make ground roasted rice powder, cook dry rice in a pan stirring so it will not burn, then grind roasted rice into a fine powder in a blender. Texture should be as semolina or fine bread crumbs.

Finely mince chicken breast (use one per person) and saute in a large skillet or wok with little or no oil if using a non-stick pan, to which lime juice, shallots, fish and oyster sauces have been added. Stir constantly over medium heat until chicken is cooked. Toss with mint leaves, chili peppers, green onions and sprinkle with ground rice.

Line a deep dish bowl or large plate with lettuce leaves and the quarters of cabbage, sliced tomatoes and cucumber. Fill center of the plate with the hot chicken preparation and serve. To eat Thai style, pull off a cabbage leaf, fill with chicken roll up like a taco and bite.

Serves one.

Safi's Chicken

4 chicken breast halves,
    skinned and boned
2 tablespoons butter
1/2 white onion, chopped
1/2 cup pine nuts
1 28-ounce can whole
    tomatoes, quartered
    and juice reserved
2 cloves of garlic,
    chopped
salt and pepper
2 tablespoons black
    olives, chopped
1/3 cup raisins
1/2 cup dry white wine
1 teaspoon cinnamon

Pound breasts with mallet until flat. Sprinkle with salt and pepper, brown in butter over medium to medium high heat in skillet. Remove and set aside. Add chopped onions to skillet and saute until translucent. Add pine nuts and continue cooking until pinenuts and onions are golden. Add quartered tomatoes with juice, garlic, olives, raisins and white wine. Bring to a boil. Add chicken, cover and reduce heat to simmer. Cook 35 to 40 minutes. Sprinkle cinnamon on top for last 10 minutes of cooking. If sauce seems too liquid remove cover for last 10 minutes of cooking. Serve over fluffy rice.

Serves four.

Curried Chicken Breasts

It was the real estate deal of any century. In 1856, the 30,000 acres surrounding the city of Monterey and much of the city itself was sold to one man - David Jacks - for a sum of $1,002.50. The entire sum was paid to attorney Delos Ashley as past payment from the city for securing title to the old pueblo properties. Despite selling thousands of acres, the city of Monterey netted not one cent. Jacks gradually amassed over 60,000 acres, truly becoming the greatest land baron in the area.

1 6-ounce can frozen
   orange juice, thawed
1 egg, beaten
1 cup coarse French
   bread crumbs
1 tablespoon
   curry powder
2 teaspoons mace
1 cup grated
   unsweetened coconut
4 chicken breast halves
4 tablespoons butter

Preheat oven to 375°. Mix juice with beaten egg. In separate bowl, flavor crumbs with mace and curry powder and stir in the coconut. Dip chicken first in juice mixture, then roll in coconut mixture. Place pieces in lightly greased baking dish or on baking sheet, and drizzle with melted butter. Bake at 375° for 45 minutes or until done. Serve with your favorite chutney and steamed rice.

Serves four.

Crispy Potato Chicken

1 large, 8-ounce potato,
   peeled
3 to 4 tablespoons
   Dijon mustard
2 cloves garlic, minced
2 whole chicken breasts,
   1 pound, skinned
   and split in half.
1 teaspoon olive oil
ground black pepper
snipped fresh parsley,
   cilantro, rosemary, or
   chives

Preheat oven to 425°. Coarsely shred the potato. Transfer to bowl of ice water; let stand 5 minutes. Stir together the mustard and garlic, mix well. Rinse chicken and pat dry. Brush or spread the mustard mixture evenly, on the meaty side of the chicken breast halves. Place the chicken bone side down in a foil lined 15x10x1 inch baking pan. Drain shredded potato thoroughly, pat dry with paper towel. Place potato in medium mixing bowl, add olive oil and toss to mix well. Top each piece of chicken with about 1/3 cup potato mixture in an even layer, forming a "skin". Sprinkle lightly with pepper. Bake at 425° oven for 45 to 50 minutes or until chicken is no longer pink and potato shreds are golden. If potatoes are not browning, broil for about 5 minutes or until golden. Sprinkle with desired herb.

Serves four.

Castroville Chicken

4 chicken half breasts,
   skinned, boned,
   pounded and cut
   into strips
1/2 pound mushrooms,
   sliced
2 cloves garlic, chopped
1/2 lemon, juiced
2 tablespoons flour
2 tablespoons butter
1/2 cup white wine
2 small jars marinated
   artichoke hearts,
   reserve marinade
1 1/2 teaspoons oregano

Brown chicken breast strips in small amount of oil in skillet over medium high heat; set aside. Melt butter in same pan. Add mushrooms, garlic, oregano and lemon juice; saute 5 minutes. Sprinkle with flour; mix well and saute 2 minutes. Add white wine and simmer until slightly thickened. Add chicken and artichokes and enough of marinade to give good consistency. Simmer 20 minutes. Serve over rice.

Serves four to six.

Grilled Chicken with Raspberry Marinade

Raspberry Marinade
1 cup pureed fresh or
 frozen unsweetened
 raspberries
1 cup raspberry vinegar
grated zest of 1 lemon
1 tablespoon minced
 shallot
2 tablespoons minced
 fresh mint

ground black pepper,
 to taste
1/3 cup olive oil

1 4-pound chicken, split
 or 4 rock Cornish
 game hens, split
fresh raspberries for
 garnish
whole mint leaves for
 garnish

To prepare marinade, combine first 6 ingredients in shallow bowl. Whisk in olive oil until well blended. Place chickens in shallow glass container and pour marinade over them. Marinate for 4 hours in refrigerator or overnight.

The chicken can be cooked either on a grill or in the oven. To cook on the grill, prepare moderate grill fire. Place chicken on grill, skin-side down. Turn chicken after 10 minutes and baste frequently with marinade. Cook 25 to 30 minutes or until juices run clear. Garnish with fresh berries and mint.

To cook in the oven, preheat oven to 350°, bake for 45 to 60 minutes until juices run clear. Baste frequently with marinade. Chicken turns deep red color - and looks beautiful when garnished. Very easy. Can be made ahead of time. Easily doubled for large parties.

Serves four.

Writer Robert Louis Stevenson sojourned briefly in Monterey while in pursuit of his lifetime love, Fanny Osborne, the wife of another man. While in Monterey, Stevenson wrote for *The Monterey California*, moving often as landlords became concerned about his illnesses. After three-and-a-half months, he was happy to leave "the tattling town" of Monterey for San Francisco, but in his writings *The Old and New Pacific Capitals* he captured the essence of the city and the lost cause of the Californios.

Crusty Chicken Breasts with Fresh Salsa

4 boneless chicken
  breast halves
1 1/2 cups fresh white
  breadcrumbs
1/2 cup fresh grated
  Parmesan cheese
1 1/2 teaspoons
  lemon zest
2 eggs, beaten

Salsa
2 large bunches arugula,
  trimmed and chopped
4 ripe tomatoes, peeled,
  seeded, and chopped
1/4 cup chopped
  red onion
2 tablespoons olive oil
2 tablespoons chopped
  fresh basil or
  2 teaspoons dried basil
1 tablespoon balsamic
  vinegar

Preheat oven to 350°. Combine breadcrumbs, Parmesan and lemon zest in shallow bowl. Place eggs in another shallow bowl. Season chicken with salt and pepper. Dip each chicken piece into egg, turning to coat completely. Dredge both sides in bread crumb mixture, pressing to adhere. Transfer chicken to baking pan. Bake in 350° degree oven for 30 minutes. Meanwhile, combine arugula, tomatoes, onion, olive oil, basil, vinegar and lemon juice. Spoon 1/4 of salsa on each chicken breast prior to serving.

Creamy Dijon Chicken Bundles

6 chicken breast halves,
   boned and skinned
4 tablespoons butter
2 to 3 shallots, minced
1/2 cup dry white wine
1/4 cup Dijon mustard
1/4 cup grained or
   country style mustard

1 cup cream
18 sheets phyllo dough,
   thawed
6 to 8 tablespoons melted
   butter for phyllo

Cut chicken into 1 inch chunks. Saute in melted butter over medium high heat for about 4 to 5 minutes until opaque but not quite fully cooked. Remove chicken to bowl. Pour off all but 1 teaspoon butter and add shallots. Saute for 1 minute. Deglaze pan with white wine. Add mustards and cream and cook over medium high heat until reduced by half or until sauce reaches thick coating consistency. Add sauce to bowl with chicken, tossing to coat.

To assemble: Preheat oven to 425°. Lay one sheet of phyllo dough on a flat surface and brush with melted butter. Repeat until you have 3 layers. Put 1/6 of the chicken mixture at the center of the shorter end. Fold edge over to cover filling. Fold in one side to seal and roll bundle over once toward opposite end. Fold in the other side and continue to roll bundle into neat cylinder. Place seam side down on baking sheet and repeat until you have 6 bundles. Bake at 425° for 5 minutes or until phyllo is golden.

Serves six.

They were known as The Big Four - Charles Crocker, Collis Huntington, Mark Hopkins and Leland Stanford. Merchants and bankers in the Gold Rush town of Sacramento, they had gambled everything on a transcontinental railroad - and reaped enormous rewards. As railroad kings they controlled California - and everything in it. Together, they formed the Pacific Improvement Company, purchasing more than 7,000 acres near Monterey from David Jacks, including much of Pacific Grove, Pebble Beach, and the site of Crocker's "most elegant seaside establishment in the world" - the Hotel Del Monte.

Mediterranean Tart

*I*t took less than six months to build the Queen of the Coast - the Hotel Del Monte. The resort's doors opened June 3, 1880, to throngs of prominent and wealthy patrons from around the globe. Guests were brought by carriage from the hotel's own Del Monte Station on the new Southern Pacific line branching from the main line at Castroville.

The Hotel del Monte amenities included salt water swimming pools, gas lights and five hundred elegant rooms. The hotel was an immediate sensation.

After an 1888 fire destroyed the original structure, a larger, three story version was built, complete with a banquet hall that could seat 1000, a race track, three polo fields, a stable of 200 horses and the area's first resort golf course.

So large was the enterprise that it published its own paper, the Del Monte <u>Wave</u>.

❦

3 tablespoons butter
1 onion, finely chopped
1 cup sliced mushrooms
1/4 teaspoon dried thyme
2 tablespoons flour
1 cup chicken stock
2 tomatoes, peeled, seeded and chopped
1 whole chicken breast, poached and cubed
1/4 pound ham, cubed
1/2 cup chopped, pitted black olives
1/2 teaspoon anchovy paste
pepper and salt
3/4 cup butter, melted
16 sheets phyllo dough
1/2 cup grated Parmesan cheese

Saute onion in 3 tablespoons of butter until soft and translucent. Add mushrooms and thyme and cook 5 minutes. Blend in flour and cook 2 to 3 minutes, stirring frequently. Add chicken stock and tomatoes and cook, stirring until thick. Reduce heat, add chicken, ham, olives and anchovy paste and simmer 5 minutes. Season and cool. Preheat oven to 300°. Grease 12x7x2 baking dish. Line dish with phyllo by alternating horizontal and vertical sheets to cover sides and bottom. Brush lightly with melted butter between each sheet to keep phyllo from drying out, using 8 sheets. Spoon filling over phyllo. Sprinkle with Parmesan cheese. Top with 8 more sheets, each brushed with butter. Trim excess. Brush top with butter several times while baking until crisp and golden. Bake one hour.

Serves four to six.

❦

Spicy Italian Chicken Stew

12 hot Italian sausages,
 cut into 1 inch pieces
4 chicken breasts, halved,
 skinned, boned and
 cut into 1 inch pieces
2 tablespoons flour
1/4 cup ground fennel
2 cups white wine
1/2 to 1 cup red
 wine vinegar
3/4 cup chicken stock
hot pepper flakes or
 chopped fresh hot
 peppers, to taste
3 to 4 green or red
 peppers, cut into 1
 inch pieces
7 to 8 garlic cloves,
 finely chopped

Saute sausage pieces over high heat until all fat is rendered. Slices should be dry. Remove from pan. Rinse with hot water. Drain. Reserve. Saute chicken pieces in remaining sausage fat until lightly brown. Chicken will cook more later. Remove from pan. Rinse with hot water. Reserve.

Over medium low heat, add flour to remaining fat in pan. Stir until roux is medium brown. Add ground fennel, 1/4 cup wine and 1/4 cup vinegar. Stir. As roux begins to thicken, continue to add rest of wine, stock and vinegar until sauce bubbles. Lower heat. Add sausages, hot peppers and 1/2 pepper pieces. Simmer, covered for 1/2 to 1 hour. Add garlic, chicken and collected juices.

At this point cooking can be stopped and refrigerated for up to 24 hours. Flavor improves, if refrigerated.

Bring stew to boil. Reduce heat. Taste for seasoning; add hot pepper flakes to taste. Simmer for 15 to 30 minutes. If sauce is too thick, add additional wine, stock or water; if too thin, add cornstarch mixed with water. Add remaining peppers. Simmer, uncovered for 15 minutes. Serve hot over pasta or rice. Easily doubled.

Serves six.

Chicken Vizcaino

1 whole chicken, about 3
   pounds, cut into
   serving sized pieces
1 cup of flour for
   dredging
4 tablespoons olive oil
2 cloves garlic, finely
   chopped
2 onions, chopped
2 green peppers, chopped
1 cup sliced mushrooms
1 cup chopped tomatoes
1 teaspoon fine herbes
   (a mixture of thyme,
   oregano, sage, basil
   rosemary, marjoram)
1/2 teaspoon salt
pepper, to taste
1/2 cup white wine

Preheat oven to 350°. Dredge chicken pieces in flour.
Heat olive oil in skillet large enough to hold chicken.
Cook chicken 8 to 10 minutes in a single layer until well
browned on all sides. Remove chicken from the skillet
and place in a baking pan. Reduce heat in skillet to
medium and add garlic, onions, green peppers, and
mushrooms, cooking until slightly browned. Add tomatoes and cook for 5 minutes. Add herbs, spices and white
wine, stirring well to combine. Pour over chicken and
bake for 1 1/2 hours at 350°.

Serves four.

Grilled Herbed Game Hens

4 Cornish game hens
2 teaspoons garlic salt
2 teaspoons ground
   pepper
1 bunch each fresh basil,
   rosemary, thyme,
   oregano, marjoram
20 cloves garlic,
   5 per bird
1 onion, quartered
1/2 cup olive oil

Wash Cornish game hens and pat dry. Sprinkle a 1/2 teaspoon of pepper into the cavity of each game hen. Add 5 garlic cloves, 1/4 of the onion, 2 tablespoons oil, and equal portions of half of the fresh herbs into the cavity of each bird. Reserve remaining herbs to dice and use on outer skin. Thoroughly rub the outside of each bird with olive oil. Sprinkle each with 1/2 teaspoon garlic salt. Evenly spread the diced fresh herbs you reserved onto each bird.

Place the birds on their sides in the middle of the grill. Close lid. After 25 minutes turn hens and cover to grill. Hens will be ready in 45 to 60 minutes or when juices run clear when thigh is pierced.

Smoked Jalapeno Game Hens

4 fresh Cornish
    game hens
8 tablespoons butter
1 8 to 10-ounce jar hot
    jalapeno pepper jelly
2 to 3 handfuls wood
    chips such as hickory
    or mesquite, soaked in
    water for 20 minutes

Clean game hens, using poultry shears or kitchen scissors. Cut along each side of the backbone to remove it completely. Flatten game hen by pressing on it with hands to break the breast bone. Light the barbecue. Soak wood chips. Melt butter and pepper jelly together.

When charcoal is hot distribute soaked wood chips on top. Immediately add game hens to grill, bone side down and cover. After cooking 15 minutes, turn hens and begin basting with butter/jelly mixture. Baste often. Cook until juices run clear when thigh is pierced with fork, approximately 35 to 45 minutes. Reheat butter/jelly mixture if it becomes too thick to baste with. Game hens should be a rich mahogany color from smoking process and shiny and moist from the jalapeno glaze. Although hot pepper jelly is used, the taste is savory but not spicy.

Serves four to six.

Roast Duck with Blackberry Sauce

Sauce
2 pounds chicken
    necks or backs
1 large onion,
    coarsely chopped
4 shallots, halved,
    unpeeled
1/2 teaspoon whole
    black peppercorns
1/4 teaspoon dried thyme
1 cup dry red wine
2 tablespoons raspberry
    vinegar (or any fruit

vinegar or red wine
    vinegar)
4 cups chicken stock
2 1/4 cups blackberries or
    boysenberries, fresh
    or frozen
blackberries for garnish

1 4 to 5 pound duck
1/4 cup plus 1 tablespoon
    unsalted butter,
    room temperature
1 tablespoon vegetable oil

Preheat oven to 400°. Place chicken necks, onion and shallots in large ovenproof saucepan or dutch oven. Roast until bones are brown, approximately 30 minutes. Remove from oven. Add peppercorns and thyme. Over medium high heat add wine and vinegar. Boil until liquid is thick, about 10 minutes. Add stock and 2 cups berries. Bring to boil. Simmer until reduced to 1 cup. Strain into medium saucepan, pressing solids to extract flavors. Refrigerate until chilled. Can be made 4 days in advance. Skim fat from sauce and bring to boil. Simmer 20 minutes until sauce is reduced to 3/4 cup. When ready to serve, return sauce to a simmer. Whisk in 1/4 cup butter. Remove from heat. Add remaining berries.

To prepare duck, preheat oven to 500°. Pat duck dry and season with salt and pepper. Place 1 tablespoon butter and vegetable oil in roasting pan. Place in oven to melt butter. Add duck, breastside down. Roast 25 minutes. Turn and bake another 45 minutes at 400°. Carve duck and serve with sauce.

Herb Roasted Turkey

Beat Giger
The Lodge at Pebble Beach

10 to 12 pound turkey
1 lemon, quartered
3 cloves garlic
2 celery ribs, cut into 2
    inch lengths
3 to 4 sprigs of parsley
2 to 3 tablespoons
    Herbs de Provence,
    (a mixture of thyme,
    marjoram, rosemary)
salt and pepper, to taste

Preheat oven to 450°. Wash turkey inside and out and dry well with paper towels. Place quartered lemon inside, rubbing the walls of the cavity. Add garlic, celery, parsley and 1 tablespoon of herbs. Truss turkey if necessary and brush outside with olive oil. Sprinkle generously with additional herbs, salt and pepper.

Oil the roasting rack and place the turkey, breast down, on the rack in a roasting pan. Bake 30 minutes, basting once after 15 minutes.

Turn turkey, breast side up, reduce heat to 325° and continue roasting. Baste with pan juices every 15 to 20 minutes. Bake approximately 15 to 20 minutes per pound, until breast meat registers 170°. Test by inserting meat thermometer in thickest part of breast, not touching bone. When done, place on warm platter and cover loosely with aluminum foil. Let sit 15 minutes before carving.

For another holiday treat serve
Jolly Holiday Egg Nog

16 eggs

1/2 cup sugar

nutmeg, to taste

1 pint rum

1/2 gallon milk

1/2 gallon half and half

1 pint whipping cream

1 quart vanilla ice cream,
    softened

1 pint brandy

1/2 pint bourbon

Beat eggs, sugar, nutmeg, half of the rum and 2 cups of milk together very well. Refrigerate overnight. On the next day add the remaining milk, half and half, remaining liquor, ice cream, and whipping cream. Stir and place in large bowl.

Serves 25, 6 ounce servings.

BREADS & BRUNCH

Pacific Grove

From its beginnings as a Methodist retreat, Pacific Grove has beckoned to those seeking solace from the ordinary. As the tent cities of summer gave way to more permanent buildings, families were drawn to the small hometown on the blue Pacific, where the beaches are safe and the water swimmable. Butterflies also find seasonal refuge in the forested parks scattered throughout the town.

The Victorian buildings call to a new generation, offering relaxation in the elegance of the past, while the morning fog off the cool ocean encourages late mornings and warm fires. Whether you bed and breakfast in your own restored home, or are visiting another, you'll want to take your time, buttering homemade bread at a Pacific Grove brunch.

Smoked Salmon Crepes

Crepes
1/2 cup flat beer
1/2 cup cold water
1 cup cold milk
4 eggs
1/2 teaspoon salt
2 cups sifted fine
    pastry flour
4 tablespoons melted
    butter

Filling
1/2 pound smoked
    salmon
1 to 2 ounces capers
8 ounces cream cheese
4 ounces sour cream

To prepare the crepes, put the liquids, eggs, and the salt into the blender. Add the flour, then the butter. Cover and blend at top speed for 1 minute. Use a rubber scraper to loosen flour that sticks to the sides of the jar. Blend for 2 or 3 seconds more. Cover and refrigerate for 2 to 4 hours.

Preheat crepe pan with a small amount of vegetable oil. Pour in batter. Tilt the pan in all directions to run the batter over the bottom of the pan. Cook for 60 to 80 seconds. Then jerk and toss the pan sharply back and forth and up and down to loosen the crepe. Lift its edges with a spatula. When the underside is a nice golden brown, turn by flipping or use spatula. Cook additional few seconds and remove from pan.

To prepare salmon filling, finely chop salmon and capers. Mix well with cream cheese and sour cream. Spread on crepes, roll up and refrigerate.

Makes 12 Crepes, 6 to 6 1/2 inches in diameter

Oatmeal Waffles

1 1/2 cups quick
   cook oatmeal
3/4 cup unsifted whole
   wheat flour
1 tablespoon sugar
1 teaspoon baking soda
2 tablespoons oil
2 cups buttermilk (or 2
   cups skim milk + 2
   teaspoons lemon juice)
1 egg
Options: cinnamon,
   nutmeg, cloves,
   1 teaspoon maple
   flavoring or
   vanilla flavoring.

Combine and mix oats, flour, sugar and baking soda. Add remaining ingredients. Stir to blend. Let stand 30 minutes. Use batter for waffles or pancakes.

Makes 8 four inch pancakes.

Custard Baked French Toast

Extra thick sliced
   French bread
6 whole eggs, beaten
3 egg yolks
1 1/2 cups sugar
1 tablespoon vanilla
   extract
Dash of nutmeg
4 cups milk
2 cups heavy cream
Cinnamon
Sliced almonds
Powdered sugar

Preheat oven to 350°. Line bottom of buttered baking dish with thick sliced bread. Make certain bread fits snugly inside baking dish. You may have to use two baking dishes to serve 8 people. Mix together eggs, sugar, vanilla, and nutmeg. Add remaining ingredients and whisk thoroughly. Pour mixture over bread. Bread will float. Sprinkle with cinnamon and sliced almonds. Bake for 1 hour at 350°. Let stand 5 minutes before cutting. Place on plate. Dust with powdered sugar and garnish with fresh fruit. Perfect for large groups, Sunday brunch and Christmas morning.

Serves eight.

In 1850 the United States Congress approved funding for navigational aids for West Coast shipping - with the result that eight lighthouses were built along the Pacific Ocean. Pacific Grove's Point Pinos Lighthouse is the second oldest of this chain, and the longest continuously operating lighthouse on the Pacific Coast.

Persimmon Bread

Make this every year around Thanksgiving during fall persimmon season in small loaf pans and wrap in colored plastic wrap for take-home "favors" from Thanksgiving dinner.

❦

Sift together:

1 3/4 cups flour

3/4 teaspoon salt

1 teaspoon baking soda

1/2 teaspoon
   ground mace

1/2 tablespoon cinnamon

1 cup sugar

1 cup persimmon puree
   (about 4 whole
   persimmons)

1/2 cup unsalted butter,
   melted

2 eggs, lightly beaten

1/3 cup cognac, brandy,
   or bourbon

1 cup walnuts, coarsely
   chopped

1 cup raisins

Preheat oven to 350°. Sift dry ingredients together and set aside. Puree persimmons in food processor (do not peel them) and set aside. Mix butter, eggs, and liquor together. Add persimmon puree and mix well. In food processor mix dry ingredients, with wet mixture, until smooth. Stir in walnuts and raisins. Grease and flour a round 1 1/2 quart pyrex bowl, or two loaf pans, filling 1/2 to 3/4 full. Bake at 350° for 1 hour. Let cool in pans.

Keeps 5 days tightly wrapped. Freezes well.

Pick persimmons that are soft, or they will be too acidic tasting.

❦

Tart Berry Muffins

1 1/2 cups all purpose
    flour
1 teaspoon baking
    powder
1/4 teaspoon salt
6 tablespoons
    unsalted butter
1 cup sugar
2 large eggs
3 teaspoons grated
    lemon peel
1/2 cup milk
1 1/2 cups fresh
    raspberries or frozen,
    thawed, drained

Preheat oven to 325°. Butter muffin tin. Combine flour, baking powder and salt in small bowl. Using electric mixer, cream butter with sugar in large bowl until light and fluffy. Add eggs one at a time, beating well after each addition. Add lemon peel. Mix in dry ingredients alternately with milk. Fold in raspberries. Spoon batter into prepared muffin pan. Bake until golden brown and toothpick inserted into center comes out clean, about 20 to 25 minutes.

Makes 18 muffins.

*T*he owner of the 7,000 acres that made up the Monterey Peninsula was a pious man. David Jacks, learning of the Methodist Church's plans to establish a seaside retreat, he donated 100 acres of land between the waterfront and Lighthouse Avenue and loaned the retreat Association $30,000 to put in streets, construct buildings and make other initial improvements.

In the summer of 1875 lots were divided, ranging from 30 by 50 feet for tents to 30 by 125 for houses, with a minimum price of $50, creating the area of Pacific Grove.

Cranberry Orange Bread

2 cups flour
1 teaspoon salt
1 teaspoon baking soda
1 teaspoon baking
   powder
1/2 cup vegetable
   shortening at
   room temperature
1 1/4 cup sugar
2 large eggs, lightly
   beaten
1/2 cup buttermilk
1/2 teaspoon vanilla
1 tablespoon grated
   orange rind
1 cup fresh whole
   cranberries

Glaze
1/8 cup orange juice
1/4 cup powdered sugar

Preheat oven to 350°. Combine dry ingredients in large bowl. In another bowl, thoroughly mix shortening, sugar, eggs, buttermilk, vanilla and orange rind. Add flour mixture; mix well. Fold in cranberries gently. Grease two 5x9x3 inch bread pans. Pour in batter. Bake 40 minutes; test with toothpick. When toothpick comes out clean, bread is done.

Make glaze by mixing orange juice and sugar; let sit until sugar dissolves. Leave bread in pans, drizzle glaze over. Remove carefully from pans; let rest on cooling rack for 30 minutes before slicing. Better the next day.

Lover's Point Bread

6 tablespoons butter
1 1/2 cups of sugar
1/4 teaspoon orange
    flavoring
1 lemon, juiced and
    rind grated
2 eggs, beaten
1 1/2 cups, plus
    1 tablespoon flour
1 1/2 teaspoons baking
    powder
1 teaspoon salt
4 shakes of ground cloves
1/2 cup milk

Preheat oven to 350°. Cream butter and 1 1/4 cups sugar. Add eggs in which the orange flavoring and the grated lemon rind have been mixed. Blend. Sift in flour, baking powder, salt and cloves and mix. Beat for 1 to 2 minutes. Pour in milk and mix. Pour mixture into a greased loaf pan. Bake at 350° for 1 hour.

Sauce: Mix the lemon juice and 1/4 cup of sugar together.

Remove loaf from oven, pour sauce slowly over the loaf while still in the pan. Leave the bread in the pan until the lemon and sugar are absorbed. Remove from pan, cool and wrap in foil. Wait 24 hours before cutting.

Although many a romance has begun at Lover's Point in Pacific Grove, the name originally came from a religious, not romantic, past.

When Pacific Grove was a religious retreat, the site was used for Methodist camp meetings. The small jut of land overlooking the Pacific Ocean became known as "Lover's of Jesus Point." By 1885, the name had officially been shortened to Lover's Point and was then, as it is now, a trysting place for smitten teenagers.

Praline Breakfast Rolls

To preserve Pacific Grove's high moral tone, deeds to all property forbade the use of intoxicating beverages and gambling - including cards, dice and billiards - with automatic cancellation of property title if violations occurred. Additional laws prohibited dancing, enforced a strict curfew on residents under 18 and required that house shades be kept up until 10 p.m. At that time, the law required that the shades be drawn and the lights extinguished.

1/2 cup butter
1 cup packed brown
    sugar
1/2 teaspoon cinnamon
1/2 cup chopped pecans
2 cups flour
2 tablespoons sugar
4 teaspoons baking
    powder
1 teaspoon salt
1/4 cup butter
1 cup milk

Preheat oven to 425°. Cream butter, brown sugar and cinnamon. Set aside. Place dry ingredients in bowl and cut in 1/4 cup butter. Add milk and mix well. Knead dough about 10 times on floured board. Roll dough into a 10 inch square. Spread brown sugar mixture over dough and sprinkle with nuts. Roll up jelly roll style and seal. Cut into 10 slices and place in greased 8x8 inch pan. Bake at 425° for 15 to 20 minutes. Invert on tray while still hot.

This is a great recipe for special breakfasts. The rolls are sweet and soft and disappear quickly!

Makes 10 rolls.

Apple Spice Muffins

1/2 cup butter

1 cup sugar

1 egg

1 cup grated apples

1 3/4 cups flour

1 teaspoon baking soda

1 teaspoon nutmeg

1/4 teaspoon ground
cloves

1 teaspoon cinnamon

1/2 teaspoon salt

1 cup chopped walnuts
or pecans

Preheat oven to 350°. Beat butter and sugar until creamy. Add egg and beat until fluffy. Mix in apples. Sift together dry ingredients and stir into batter mixture until well blended. Stir in nuts. Spoon into greased muffin cups to 2/3 full. Bake 18 minutes at 350° or until top springs back.

Makes 18 muffins.

To keep out tradesmen and unruly elements, a fence encircled Pacific Grove, with a padlocked gate across the road. Residents had to hike to the retreat office for a key to enter the city. In the early 1880's, State Senator Benjamin Langford grew tired of the rigmarole involved in getting to his summer home. Arriving one evening with his family, he took out an ax, smashing the gate. It was never rebuilt.

Harvest Walnut Loaf

1 tablespoon yeast
5 tablespoons honey
1 1/2 cups warm water
2 cups toasted walnuts
4 tablespoons olive oil
2 teaspoons kosher salt
4 to 5 cups
   unbleached flour

Preheat oven to 400°. Dissolve yeast and honey in warm water. Grind walnuts in food processor until very fine and paste begins to form. Reserve. Combine dissolved yeast, 2 tablespoons olive oil and salt in bowl of heavy duty mixer. Add 3 cups flour, beat until smooth. Add walnuts. Gradually add remaining flour and beat about 5 minutes. If using food processor, put flour in first, add yeast, salt and oil, then walnuts, and process until dough cleans of bowl. Transfer to a lightly floured board, knead briefly and place in a bowl oiled with remaining 2 tablespoons olive oil. Cover and let rise until doubled, approximately 1 1/2 to 2 hours. Punch down and shape into two round loaves. Let rise 1/2 hour.

Bake, preferably on a preheated baking stone, at 400° for 40 minutes.

Gnocchi Rolls

1 package yeast
1/2 cup lukewarm water
1 teaspoon sugar
2/3 cup margarine or
    butter
1/2 cup sugar
1 teaspoon salt
1 cup instant mashed
    potatoes
1 cup scalded milk
2 eggs
6 to 7 cups flour

Preheat oven to 350°. Dissolve yeast and 1 teaspoon sugar in the lukewarm water. Pour into a large bowl and add all other ingredients. Mix and then knead on lightly floured surface. Put in greased bowl and let rise until doubled. Punch down and break into balls. Place in greased 9x13 inch baking pan and let rise until doubled. Bake at 350°, 25 minutes until golden.

Makes 15 to 18 rolls.

Known as Butterfly Town, U.S.A., Pacific Grove is the winter home for thousands of Monarch butterflies. The orange and black butterflies wing their way each fall to the coastal town, traveling from as far away as the Rocky Mountains. On warm days, the Monarchs flutter about, but as the fog rolls in, the butterflies can be seen hanging in clusters on the branches and leaves of their chosen trees.

Children in Pacific Grove annually take to the streets to celebrate the Monarch's migration. Dressed as trees and insects, featuring bright costumes and wings of black and gold, the children parade through the town each October, along with their parents and throngs of local residents, to celebrate the butterflies' return.

Raised Oatmeal Rolls

Pacific Grove's famed "purple carpet" began as a method of keeping out the noxious poison oak.

In 1938, Hayes Perkins began renting a cottage near the waterfront. He was appalled that the town's children playing along the coast caught poison oak. Immune to the plant's poison himself, he began ripping out the weed, but needed something to plant in its place. On his worldwide travels he had seen the ability of the South African mesembryanthemum to crowd out weeds. He planted the purple flowering plant, smothered the poison oak, and left a colorful shoreline at the entrance to the city.

1 package dry yeast
1/2 cup lukewarm water
1 cup scalded milk
3 cups vegetable
    shortening
1/4 cup sugar
2 teaspoons salt
1 cup cooked oatmeal
4 1/2 to 5 cups sifted
    all purpose flour
3/4 cup melted shortening

Stir yeast into lukewarm water. Pour scalded milk over shortening, sugar, and salt. Stir occasionally until shortening melts; cool to lukewarm. Stir in oatmeal and 1 cup of the flour. Add yeast and enough additional flour to make a soft dough. Knead on lightly floured surface until smooth and satiny, about 10 minutes. Form dough into a ball; place in greased bowl and brush with melted shortening.

Cover; let rise in a warm place until double in size, about 1 hour. Punch dough down, cover and let stand 10 minutes. Shape into 36 rolls or buns; place in greased muffin or baking pans. Brush with melted shortening; cover and let rise until double in bulk, about 45 minutes. Bake in a preheated 400° oven for 15 to 20 minutes or until rolls are nicely browned. Remove from pans immediately.

Makes 3 dozen rolls.

Golden Holiday Rolls

1 cup shortening
1/2 cup sugar
1 cup boiling water
1/2 cup All-Bran cereal
1 teaspoon salt
2 eggs, well beaten
2 envelopes dry yeast
1 cup warm water
7 cups flour,
    approximately
1/4 cups melted butter

Place shortening, sugar, All-Bran and salt in a large glass bowl. Pour the boiling water over this mixture and stir to melt the shortening. Add the beaten eggs. Dissolve the yeast in the warm water and add to mixture. Stir lightly. Add flour until the mixture has the consistency of cake batter, approximately 3 to 4 cups. Let rise for 2 hours. Add more flour until the dough forms a ball and then place on bread board and add more flour, while lightly kneading, until the dough can be rolled and cut.

Cut in two to three inch circles, dip in butter, fold over and place in baking dish. At this point the rolls can be refrigerated overnight or frozen. Let rise 2 hours before baking. Bake at 400° for 20 minutes.

Makes 4 dozen.

Polenta Cheese Bread

The historic past of Pacific Grove is relived each year during the city's "Good Old Days," featuring antique cars, arts and crafts fairs, parades, and a tour of the city's restored Victorian homes. Many of the vintage homes, restored both inside and out, are open to the public, each displaying a special "Heritage Plaque," telling when the house was built and naming the original owners.

1 package dry yeast
2 tablespoons sugar
1 cup warm water
4 ounces sharp Cheddar
    cheese, cut into
    small cubes
3 1/2 cups flour,
    approximately
1/2 cup polenta or
    yellow cornmeal
1 teaspoon salt
1 egg

Preheat oven to 375°. Mix yeast and 1 teaspoon sugar with water, and let sit until foamy.

In a food processor, fitted with plastic dough blade or steel blade, combine cheese, 3 1/4 cup flour, remaining sugar, polenta and salt; process until cheese is finely chopped. Add egg and, with motor running, pour in the yeast mixture in a steady stream. Run the machine for 45 seconds to knead dough. It should be sticky, but if too wet add more flour, 1 tablespoon at a time. If too dry add warm but not hot water, 1 teaspoon at a time.

Shape dough into a smooth ball, turn over in a greased bowl, cover with plastic wrap and let rise in a warm place until doubled in size, about 1 to 1 1/2 hours.

Punch down, turn out, and shape into smooth ball. Place on a greased baking sheet and let rise for about 1 hour. Sprinkle top with a tablespoon of flour and bake in a preheated 375° oven until well browned; about 35 minutes.

DESSERTS

Carmel

The sun drops, an orange splash on the blue horizon. The sky turns purple as the last rays wind through the twisted pines that line the streets. The end of the day has come to Carmel-by-the-Sea.

Special endings are everyday occurrences in Carmel. The one-square-mile town cherishes its uniqueness, its quaint charm, and its commitment to remain a residential village. The former home of artists and writers, including George Sterling, Jack London, and Robinson Jeffers now inspires future cultural endeavors, while still attracting the tourists anxious to peruse the unique shops lining Ocean Avenue. The city continually considers the needs of residents and those of the business sector, offering in the end a balance for the best of both. So weigh your options and anticipate beautiful endings, a delicious and beautiful finale to your culinary experience.

Phyllo Napoleons

4 sheets phyllo dough,
   thawed
3 to 4 tablespoons
   melted butter
4 tablespoons .
   superfine sugar
1 cup cream
1 teaspoon vanilla
   (or substitute 1
   tablespoon liqueur
   such as Triple Sec,
   etc., if desired)
1 cup fresh berries,
   whole if small or sliced
   if large
1/4 cup powdered sugar,
   plus more for dusting

Lay one sheet of phyllo dough on a flat surface. Lightly brush with melted butter. Sprinkle on 1 teaspoon of sugar. Repeat to make 4 layers. Cut phyllo with sharp knife into six strips lengthwise and four strips widthwise to make 24 rectangles 4x2 inches. Place on baking sheet and bake at 350° for 5 minutes. Turn rectangles over carefully and bake for 5 more minutes or until deep golden brown. Cool.

To make filling: Whip cream, adding vanilla, or liqueur of choice, and powdered sugar. Fold in berries.

To assemble: Use half of whipped cream mixture to top 8 of the phyllo rectangles spreading cream level. Top each with a second phyllo rectangle and spread with remaining cream. Lay a third rectangle on the top and dust well with powdered sugar. Serve at once or chill covered up to one hour.

Serves eight.

*O*n Christmas Eve, 1771, the Carmel Mission of San Carlos Borromeo, the second mission in California, was dedicated by Father Junipero Serra, the founder of the California mission system. Serra was attracted by the fertile soil, the fresh water and the proximity of the Indian population whose souls he was determined to save.

For years, only the Franciscan fathers and the Ohlone Indians enjoyed the beautiful coastline on the Rio Carmelo. Cut off by the hills from booming Monterey, the quiet country mission continued to welcome travelers, raise cattle, and convert the native population. Its serenity made the mission Serra's favorite, and after his death in 1784, he was buried at the Mission San Carlos. The mission was later completed in 1797.

Ollalieberry Cobbler

The city of Carmel by the Sea began in 1888 when Monterey developer S. J. Duckworth saw the possibility of developing the property as a Catholic summer retreat, similar to the Methodist retreat at Pacific Grove. Capitalizing on the renovation of the Carmel mission, he rushed to divide lots without regard for trees, ravines or gullies and within two months, 200 lots had sold.

Duckworth even built an 18 room hotel complete with a bath house equipped with a glassed in observation platform and outdoor showers. Twenty-five cents rented a bathing suit, towel, and dressing room.

Unfortunately for Duckworth, the real estate venture went bankrupt.

1/2 cup butter
2 cups ollalieberries
   (1 pint if frozen fruit)
1 cup sugar
1 cup milk
1 cup flour
1 teaspoon baking powder
Vanilla ice cream

Preheat oven to 350°. Melt butter in 8x8 inch baking dish. Add ollalieberries . Mix the sugar, milk, flour and baking powder; pour over fruit. Bake in 350° oven for 40 minutes or until brown on top. Serve warm with vanilla ice cream on top. Blueberries, blackberries, or peaches may be substituted for the ollalieberries.

Serves six to eight.

Fresh Berry Shortbread Tart

Shortbread
1/4 pound butter -
   room temperature
3 tablespoons sugar
1 1/3 cups flour
1/2 teaspoon salt
1 teaspoon vanilla
1 egg yolk and
   2 teaspoons
   cold water

Custard
3 tablespoons flour
1/4 cup sugar

1 egg yolk
1/2 cup milk
2 teaspoons orange
   liqueur

Berries
1 1/2 pints strawberries,
   sliced lengthwise
1 cup blueberries or
   blackberries
1/3 cup seedless
   raspberry jelly
1 teaspoon orange liqueur

Shortbread: Preheat oven to 375°. Cream butter and sugar. Beat in flour and add remaining ingredients. Form into ball and chill 30 minutes. Roll out dough and press into bottom of 9-inch tart pan with removable bottom. Prick all over with fork. Chill 30 minutes. Cover with foil and bake at 375° for 15 minutes. Remove foil and bake 10 to 15 minutes more until light brown. Cool in pan.

Custard: Combine flour and sugar in saucepan. Beat in egg yolk. Stir in milk. Cook over low heat and stir until it boils and thickens. Boil 2 minutes while stirring. Press through sieve and add liqueur. Cool in refrigerator. Spread over cooked tart shell.

Berries: Spread strawberries around outer edge of tart in concentric circles. Place blueberries in center. Melt jelly with liqueur. Brush over the berries. Chill and serve. Serves eight.

In 1908 James Franklin Devendorf traded in property he held in Stockton to acquire the Carmel land originally developed by S.J. Duckworth. Devendorf and his partner San Francisco Attorney Frank Powers planted trees down the middle of Ocean Avenue to prevent erosion and counted on the natural beauty of the surroundings to bring buyers. Putting Duckworth's old hotel on rollers, Devendorf pushed the hotel five blocks down to become the nucleus of the present-day Pine Inn. The new inn opened on July 4, 1903, amid much fanfare to guests and prospective buyers escaping the heat of the San Joaquin Valley. For as little as $100, with five dollars down and five dollars a month, buyers, brought by open carriage on an hour-long ride over dirt roads from the Monterey depot, could purchase lots in the new town. Within a year, the city had 75 residences and was the year round home for 32 families.

Apricot Souffle

Michael Jones
A Moveable Feast

M ichael Jones is the proprietor of A Moveable Feast catering company in Carmel Valley. Michael is a classically trained French chef who has been working at the cutting edge of California cuisine for nearly twenty years. His work features locally grown organic produce, imaginative and attractive presentations, and creative menus that reflect a wide variety of culinary influences.

Souffle
8 ounces extra fancy
    dried apricots
1 cup sugar
white wine
16 egg whites
12 egg yolks
powdered sugar

Ice Cream Sauce
1 quart premium vanilla
    ice cream
4 ounces Myers rum

Preheat oven to 425°. Butter a souffle dish and sprinkle with sugar until well covered.

To prepare souffle, place apricots in a blender with sugar. Add enough wine to cover apricots and sugar. Do not blend yet. Let sit overnight. Blend apricots until smooth. Add yolks. Whisk whites by hand until soft peaks form. Fold apricot mixture into whites. Pour into souffle dish, 3/4 full. Put dish in oven and turn temperature down to 375°. Bake for 20 to 25 minutes. Sprinkle with powdered sugar. Serve with ice cream sauce.

To prepare ice cream sauce, place ice cream in a stainless steel bowl, add rum and place in freezer. Over the course of several hours, cut rum into the ice cream until smooth. Pass on the side with apricot souffle.

Serves eight.

Frosty Strawberry Torte

Crust
1 cup flour
1/2 cup firmly packed
    brown sugar
1/2 cup finely
    chopped walnuts
1/2 cup unsalted butter,
    melted

Filling
4 egg whites
1 cup heavy cream
2 cups fresh strawberries,
    sliced (frozen may
    be used)
1 cup granulated sugar
2 tablespoons lemon juice

Preheat oven to 350°. Stir together flour, brown sugar, walnuts and butter. Spread evenly in 9x13 inch pan. Bake at 350° for 20 minutes, stirring occasionally. Remove from oven and cool. Remove 1/3 of crumb mixture and reserve. Beat egg whites until peaks form - set aside. Whip the cream to peaks. To the cream, add berries, sugar, and lemon juice. Fold in egg whites. Spoon into baking dish and top with remaining crumbs. Freeze, then thaw slightly before serving. Garnish with fresh berries. A wonderful make-ahead dessert to serve at large gatherings.

Serves sixteen.

Tangerine & Custard Crepe

Yann Lusseau
Casanova Restaurant

Crepe Batter
1 cup all purpose flour
1/2 cup buckwheat flour
1 egg, beaten
1 teaspoon salt
1 tablespoon sugar
1/2 quart milk

Pastry Cream
2 cups milk
1/3 cup sugar
3 large egg yolks
1/4 cup corn starch
1 vanilla bean, split
    and scraped
zest of 1 orange

Tangerine Filling
8 teaspoons sugar
4 teaspoons butter
4 navel oranges, peeled
    and sectioned
pastry cream
vanilla ice cream, optional
1/2 cup Grand Marnier,
    warmed

To prepare crepe batter sift together flour. In a mixing bowl, mix all dry ingredients together with a whisk. Add the egg. Gradually add the milk while mixing constantly, until batter is smooth. Refrigerate overnight. May be kept in the refrigerator up to 4 days.

Pour 1/3 cup of crepe batter into a hot crepe pan. Spread evenly by tilting the pan. Cook over medium heat until first side is cooked, golden/brown color. Flip with a spatula. When second side is cooked, flip the crepe onto a clean towel and cover with an additional towel to prevent dryness. Crepes may be made ahead of time so that you can enjoy dessert with your guests. Makes 20 crepes.

(Continued on next page)

For pastry cream, combine milk, half the sugar, and vanilla bean in large saucepan. Bring to a boil over high heat. In a separate mixing bowl, using a whisk mix together remaining half of sugar with the corn starch, add the egg yolks and beat until the mix turns pale yellow. The beating prevents the sugar from burning the egg yolks. Pour a small quantity of the boiling milk onto the egg yolk mixture and mix well. Pour entire mixture back into the sauce pan and cook over medium heat stirring constantly with whisk. Make sure the mixture does not stick to the bottom of the pan. Once it starts boiling stir an additional 2 minutes. Stir constantly the entire time. Remove from heat and transfer to mixing bowl. Add orange zest and cover with plastic wrap.

To serve, reheat crepe in crepe pan over medium heat. Top with 1 teaspoon butter, 2 teaspoons sugar, 1 large tablespoon pastry cream and four orange segments. Fold the crepe in half and serve it on a warm plate with remaining orange segments. After all crepes are assembled pour some warm Grand Marnier on each one, add a scoop of vanilla ice cream, if desired, and for the grand finale flambe.

Poached Pears in Zinfandel

8 firm pears such as bosc

Poaching Liquid
1/2 cup sugar
3/4 to 1 bottle Zinfandel
   or other dry red wine
1 2" cinnamon stick

4 to 6 strips of lemon
   zest, the yellow skin
   without the white pith

Whipped Cream
1 cup heavy cream,
   whipped
1 tablespoon sugar
1 teaspoon vanilla extract

Select a saucepan in which the pears will just fit when standing upright. In it heat the wine, sugar, cinnamon stick, and lemon zest until the sugar has dissolved. Peel the pears. Carefully core them from the base making sure to leave the stem attached. Cut a thin slice from the bottom so the pears can stand up straight. Immerse them in the poaching syrup adding more wine if necessary to cover. Cover and poach until tender 20 to 45 minutes, depending on the variety and ripeness.

Let the pears cool uncovered in the syrup to absorb as much flavor as possible. Remove them from the syrup and refrigerate. Strain the poaching liquid and reduce until thick. Let cool.

Whip the cream with the sugar and vanilla extract. Spoon the whipped cream into the hollowed out core area of the cooked pears. Place on individual serving dishes or together in a shallow glass bowl and spoon the cooled poaching syrup over them.

The pears can be cooked 24 hours before serving and kept tightly covered in the refrigerator before filling.

Serves eight.

Macadamia Nut Torte with Pineapple Mousse

Torte
2 1/2 cups sugar
2 3/4 cups flour
1 cup butter
2 large eggs
1 cup whipping cream
1 large egg white
2 1/2 cups whole roasted
    macadamia nuts

Pineapple Mousse
1 cup sugar
1 8 ounce can crushed
    pineapple
1 pint whipping cream,
    whipped
5 egg whites, beaten to
    soft peaks

Torte: Preheat oven to 325°. In food processor, mix 1/2 cup of the sugar with the flour; work in butter until fine crumbs form. Add eggs and mix into ball. Press 2/3 of pastry over bottom and all the way up the sides of an 8 inch springform pan. Chill. Roll remaining pastry to 9 inch circle. Chill. Pour the remaining 2 cups sugar into large frying pan and place over medium high heat. Stir until sugar melts and just turns amber. Pour in cream; sugar will harden. Cook, stirring until sugar melts and sauce is smooth. Remove from heat. Stir in nuts. Let cool 15 minutes, then spoon into pastry shell. Place top crust over and seal edges with fork. Brush top lightly with beaten egg white. Bake 1 hour at 325° until golden brown. Serve with pineapple mousse on side.

Pineapple Mousse: In large bowl, add sugar to pineapple. Gently fold in whipped cream and egg whites. Freeze covered. Thaw before serving.

Can be made 2 days ahead. Great dinner party dessert to serve when fresh fruits are not in season.

Serves six to eight.

Life in Carmel in the 1920's and 1930's was both carefree and communal. Villagers might meet each other at all times of the day or night in all kinds of dress. Author Mary Austin would roam the woods dressed as an Indian princess or in Greek robes. Each day, city residents would greet each other in their bathrobes at the milk stations - sets of shelves set up at two-block intervals where residents would leave money at night and pick up their milk in the morning.

White Chocolate Creme Brulee

*I*t was a love affair that first brought poet George Sterling to Carmel. The leader of a small colony of artists in San Francisco and a member of the city's Bohemian Club, he had become entranced with writer Mary Hunter Austin. When Austin wanted to gather information about the Mission San Carlos for a novel, Sterling offered to take her to Carmel. Both were married, but the early summer of 1905 was an "idyllic interlude" according to Austin's autobiography, as the two wandered along the coast "looking for pitch pine and bee trees."

The two parted, vowing to return to the scenic coast and by the end of June, Sterling returned to build a house, moving in with his wife, Carrie. ❦

1 whole egg
3 egg yolks
1/4 cup sugar
2 cups whipping cream
4 ounces white chocolate,
    finely chopped
1/2 teaspoon vanilla
4 teaspoons sugar

Preheat oven to 325°, with rack in center of oven. Whisk eggs and 2 tablespoons sugar in medium bowl. Bring cream and remaining sugar to simmer in heavy medium saucepan. Reduce heat. Gradually add chopped chocolate to cream mixture and whisk until smooth. Gradually whisk hot chocolate mixture into egg mixture. Mix in vanilla. Ladle custard into four 6 to 9 ounce custard cups. Place cups in large baking pan. Add enough hot water to pan to come halfway up sides of cups. Bake until sharp knife comes out dry when inserted into center of custards. They will continue to firm as they cool. Remove from water and cool. Cover and refrigerate overnight.

To serve, preheat broiler and sprinkle 1 teaspoon of sugar over each custard. Broil until sugar caramelizes, watching carefully, about 2 minutes. Serve hot or cold.

Serves four.

❦

Cappuccino Souffle

Butter and granulated
    sugar to coat
    souffle dish
2 cups whole milk
2 tablespoons coffee
    liqueur
1 tablespoon cognac
    or brandy
2 tablespoons instant
    coffee granules

1/2 ounce unsweetened or
    semi-sweet chocolate
1 teaspoon vanilla
1/4 cup unsalted butter
2 rounded tablespoons
    flour
1/4 cup sugar
6 eggs, separated

Preheat oven to 350°. Butter a 1 quart souffle dish. Fold a piece of waxed paper large enough to reach around dish into 1/3's. Form a 2 inch collar around the souffle dish. Butter inside of collar and tie with kitchen twine. Sprinkle dish and collar with sugar and butter.

Combine milk, liqueurs, coffee granules, chocolate and vanilla extract in saucepan and cook over low heat until chocolate is melted. Set aside. Melt butter, add flour and stir, cooking until bubbly. Gradually add chocolate mixture and sugar whisking until smooth. Bring to boil and cook until thickened. Pour into bowl. Beat in egg yolks one at a time carefully as not to curdle the yolks. Beat egg whites until soft and glossy. Gently fold into chocolate mixture. Spoon into prepared souffle dish, mounding in the center. Bake 25 minutes.

Good served with creme anglaise or vanilla custard sauce. See custard sauce on page 232.

Serves six.

Raspberry Souffle

The disastrous earth quake that leveled San Francisco on April 18, 1906, boosted the artist population of Carmel. Many of George Sterling's friends drifted down the coast, seeking refuge from the devastated city. Among the many guests were Jack London and his wife Charmian.

While others frolicked on the Carmel coast, London stuck to a strict work schedule, writing a thousand words a day and getting editorial help from his friends.

After work the group of artists and writers might meet on the beach for one of Sterling's impromptu abalone or mussel parties, discussing the international Socialist movement, their work, or just the beauty of the town until late into the night. The bohemian behavior of the artistic residents caused their fellow city dwellers to rename the beachfront "The Barbary Coast."

Vanilla custard sauce
1 1/2 cups whole milk
1 1/2 teaspoons vanilla
4 egg yolks
3 tablespoons sugar

Souffle
1 12-ounce jar
    raspberry jam
1/2 lemon, juiced
5 egg whites
1 teaspoon sugar
2 tablespoons Framboise,
    optional

To prepare custard sauce, combine milk, vanilla, egg yolks and sugar in saucepan. Heat over low heat, stirring constantly until mixture coats the back of a spoon. Pour into sauce boat and cover with plastic wrap.

To prepare souffle, preheat oven to 375°. Butter and sugar a 1 quart souffle dish. Melt the jam with the lemon juice. Strain to remove the seeds. Keep warm.

Stiffly beat the egg whites, beat in the sugar and continue beating until whites are glossy. Fold about 1/4 of the whites into the warm jam mixture. Mix thoroughly, then add to remaining whites, folding in as lightly as possible. Pour into prepared souffle dish. Bake the souffle at 375° for 15 to 20 minutes, until puffed and brown. Serve at once, with vanilla custard sauce passed separately.

Wonderful to make any time of year, especially when fresh raspberries are unavailable, since the jam yields the same flavor.

Serves six.

Chocolate Raspberry Cheesecake

Crust
25 chocolate cookie
    wafers, crushed
1/2 cup melted butter

Filling
2 8 ounce packages cream
    cheese, softened
1 cup sugar
1/2 cup sour cream
4 eggs
1 cup (1/2 pint) fresh
    raspberries
1 ounce raspberry liqueur

Preheat oven to 350°. In food processor combine cookie wafers and butter. When completely mixed, press into a 9" springform pan, covering bottom and sides.

To softened cream cheese, add sugar and mix well. Add eggs, sour cream, raspberries and liqueur. You may choose to add drop of red food coloring for bright-pink color.

Bake 40 minutes. Cool in oven turned off, for 40 minutes. Refrigerate. Then garnish by melting semisweet chocolate in double boiler, then drizzling in wild lines over top with spoon. Serve with fresh raspberries.

Special and can be made a day ahead.

Serves eight to ten.

*"O*h! some folks boast
        of quail on toast,
Because they think it's tony:
But I'm content to owe my rent
        and live on abalone.

"The more we take, the more
        they make
In deep-sea matrimony;
Race suicide cannot betide
The fertile abalone.

"Oh! some think the Lord
        is fat
And some think he is bony;
But as for me I think that He
Is like an abalone."

        – The Abalone Song,
as sung by George Sterling,
Jack London and other
artists in Carmel's Barbary
Coast colony.

Cabrillo Almond Triangles

It was the artists who first called attention to the beauty and seclusion of Carmel, beginning the city's never-ending struggle between the preservationists and the business sector. Concern over the development of the village prompted residents to vote for incorporation in 1916, and locals have struggled to keep the town the same ever since. In 1929, the battle reached a rousing climax with the election of journalist Perry Newberry who ran with the slogan, "Keep Carmel Off the Map!"

"If you think a glass factory is of greater importance than a sand dune, or a millionaire than an artist, or a mansion than a little brown cottage. If you truly want Carmel to become a boosting, hustling, wideawake, lively metropolis, DON'T VOTE FOR PERRY NEWBERRY."

– part of Perry Newberry's campaign platform in the 1929 Carmel City Council race.

1 pound butter, room
  temperature
3/4 cup granulated sugar
1/2 teaspoon salt
3/4 teaspoon almond
  extract
1 egg
2 3/4 cups flour
1 cup brown sugar
1/3 cup honey
1/4 cup heavy cream
1 pound sliced almonds
  (approximately
  5 1/4 cups)

Line 15x10 inch jelly roll pan with foil. Beat 1/2 pound butter, 1/2 cup granulated sugar, salt and almond extract. Beat in egg and then flour. Press dough into pan and push up sides. Refrigerate, at least 1 hour. Heat oven to 375°. Prick dough with fork and bake 10 minutes.

In a saucepan, combine brown sugar, honey, the remaining 1/2 pound of butter and the remaining 1/4 cup granulated sugar and cook over low heat, stirring occasionally, until sugar dissolves. Bring mixture to a boil without stirring and boil 3 minutes. Remove from heat and stir in cream and almonds. Spread over crust. Bake until bubbling, 10 to 15 minutes. Cool and cut into triangles.

Makes 80 triangles.

Apricot Chocolate Bars

Cookie
1/2 cup unsalted butter,
  room temperature
1/4 cup sifted
  powdered sugar
1 cup flour
1/8 teaspoon salt

Filling
1 cup chopped dried
  apricots
3 tablespoons sugar
1/4 cup apricot wine
1 teaspoon finely
  chopped orange zest

Topping
2 squares (2 ounces)
  semi-sweet chocolate

Preheat oven to 350°. Line bottom and sides of an 8x8x2 inch baking pan with foil. Set aside.

Cookie: In a medium bowl, beat butter with sugar until combined. Beat in flour and salt. Press firmly into bottom of prepared pan. Bake 20 to 25 minutes or until lightly browned. Cool in pan on rack.

Filling: In a medium saucepan, combine all ingredients for filling and bring to a boil. Cook over medium heat 15 minutes or until apricots are very soft. Place in a food processor and cover. Puree until smooth. Let cool.

Topping: Melt chocolate in top of a double boiler set over simmering water or place in a 1 cup glass measuring cup and microwave on medium for 2 to 3 minutes, stirring twice.

Brush cooled cookie with most of the chocolate; let set. Spread apricot puree over chocolate. Drizzle remaining chocolate over apricot layer in a zig-zag pattern. Let set. Lift cookie from pan with foil. Set on counter. Cut into 1 inch bars.

Makes 2 1/2 dozen bars.

Bargetto winery was founded on the day prohibition was repealed, December 5, 1933 by Phillip and John Bargetto.

Today Bargetto Winery is operated by the third generation and is dedicated to producing award winning chardonnays, cabernets and pinot noirs. They are also well known for their fruit wines such as rapsberry and peach.

The tasting room in Cannery Row has become a mainstay to tourists as well as locals.

Oatmeal Lace Cookies

1/2 cup flour
1/4 teaspoon baking
   powder
1/2 cup sugar
1/2 cup quick cooking
   oatmeal
2 tablespoons heavy
   cream
2 tablespoons light corn
   syrup
1/3 cup butter, melted

Preheat oven to 350°. Sift the first three ingredients together. Add the rest of ingredients and mix well. Drop teaspoons of dough on ungreased cookie sheet 4 inches apart. Bake at 350° for 8 to 10 minutes or until golden. Let stand a few seconds before removing. If left too long on cookie sheet, put back in oven for a few seconds.

Makes 2 1/2 dozen cookies.

Coconut Crisps

1 cup butter
1 cup firmly packed
   brown sugar
1 cup sugar
1 teaspoon vanilla
2 eggs
1 1/2 cups flour
1 teaspoon salt
1 teaspoon baking soda
3 cups quick cooking
   rolled oats
3/4 cup flaked coconut

Preheat oven to 350°. Cream butter and sugars until fluffy. Stir in vanilla, add eggs, one at a time, beating after each addition. Sift flour, salt and baking soda together. Add to creamed mixture. Stir in oats and coconut. Drop by teaspoonfuls about 2" apart on well greased cookie sheet. Bake at 350° for 8 to 10 minutes. These cookies freeze well.

Makes 6 dozen cookies.

In addition to Sterling, Austin and London, other artists began migrating to the new town of Carmel, including photographer Arnold Genthe, pioneer painter Chris Jorgenson, writers Upton Sinclair, Alice MacGowan, Grace MacGowan Cooke, and Sinclair Lewis, and actor Herbert Heron Peet, founder of the Forest Theater. It was Heron (as he was known) who sold developer Devendorf on the idea of an outdoor theater and the Carmel businessman gave the Forest Theater Society an entire wooded block free of charge for thespian use. The opening performance at California's first open-air theater was "David," with Heron in the title role.

Vanilla Crescents

1/2 pound butter

2 teaspoons vanilla
  extract

7 tablespoons granulated
  sugar

2 cups flour

1 cup grated walnuts,
  can finely chop in the
  food processor

Vanilla Sugar

1 vanilla bean

2 cups powdered sugar

At least one day before preparing cookies, make vanilla sugar: slit open vanilla bean and add powdered sugar. Keep tightly closed in a jar, shaking from time to time.

Preheat oven to 350°. Cream butter, vanilla extract and granulated sugar in the mixer. Add flour and walnuts to mixture and beat until well blended. Roll dough into ropes and shape into 72 crescents approximately 1 3/4 inches long and 1/2 inch wide. Bake at 350° until slightly brown, about 12 minutes. Cool slightly. Using 1/2 cup at a time, put powdered sugar on a small plate. Gently roll each cookie in the sugar until coated on all sides.

They make great Christmas cookies and freeze very well.

Makes 6 dozen cookies.

Biscotti Duet

Master Recipe
2 cups all purpose
   flour
1/2 teaspoon baking
   powder
1 cup sugar plus 1
   teaspoon for sprinkling
3 tablespoons cold
   unsalted butter, diced
1/4 teaspoon salt
2 large eggs
1 egg yolk

Coffee Cashew Biscotti
3/4 cup unsalted, lightly
   roasted cashews
1 tablespoon instant
   coffee granules,
   preferably espresso

Almond Biscotti
3/4 cup whole almonds
1 1/2 teaspoons almond
   extract

Preheat oven to 350°. In a food processor combine the flour, baking powder, salt and 2/3 cup of sugar. Add the diced butter and combine until mixture resembles coarse meal. Add the eggs and pulse to combine.

Separate the mixture into two bowls. Into one add the coffee and cashews. Into the other add the almond extract and almonds. Mix well.

Lightly butter a baking sheet. Using your hands, separate the mixture in each bowl in half again. Pat each quarter into an 8" log. Place the logs on the baking sheet, flattening each with your hand to a width of 2". Sprinkle the tops with the remaining teaspoon of sugar. Bake for about 20 minutes, or until golden brown. Carefully transfer the logs to a rack to cool slightly, 5 to 10 minutes.

Place the logs on a work surface. Using a sharp knife, in a quick motion slice each log on the diagonal 3/4" thick. Place the biscotti cut side down on the baking sheet and return to the oven for 15 to 20 minutes more, just until they begin to color, turning once. If you prefer chewy biscotti cook less, for crispy biscotti bake slightly longer. Transfer to a rack to cool completely.

Makes 3 dozen cookies.

The artists enlivened the area with their presence as much as with their paint. Surrealist Salvador Dali both worked and played on the Monterey Peninsula, including staging a soiree in the 1940s for developer Samuel F.B. Morse entitled "Night in a Surrealist Forest." For the event, Dali had wild animals shipped down from the San Francisco Zoo to roam wild in the Del Monte Forest. His only regret was that the zoo was unable to send a giraffe.

Fresh Apple Cake

The conflicts between the business community and the city residents continued to escalate, as the city council strove to regulate visitor-serving businesses almost out of existence. Almost all agreed that "fast-food" restaurants did not fit the character of Carmel, but as the city government strove to control the number of art galleries, jewelry shops, bookstores, clothing stores, and even outlawed ice cream cones, it was clear that the two elements were never to agree.

In every Western, a hero comes to save the town, so in 1984 actor Clint Eastwood rode in on the scene, a long-time city resident with substantial business interests in the town. As Carmel's most famous mayor, Eastwood tried to reconcile the opposing groups, defining areas of agreement and agreeing to disagree on other issues. Promoting compromise, Eastwood used his fame and connections to preserve his hometown while moving the city toward the 21st century.

2 cups sugar
3 cups flour
1 1/2 teaspoons baking soda
1/2 teaspoon salt
1/2 teaspoon ground cloves
1/2 teaspoon nutmeg
2 teaspoons ground cinnamon
2 teaspoons vanilla extract
1 cup oil
3 eggs
3 cups chopped apple
1 cup chopped pecans

Glaze
1/2 cup butter
1/4 cup water
8 to 16 ounces powdered sugar
2 teaspoons ground cinnamon

Preheat oven to 350°. Sift dry ingredients together. Add the liquid ingredients, stirring well to combine. Add the chopped apples and nuts. Bake in large lightly oiled bundt pan at 350° for about 1 hour and 15 minutes, or until cake tester comes out clean.

Glaze: Melt butter, add water, sugar and cinnamon. Stir and blend well. Pour over cake while it is still hot.

Serves ten to twelve.

*Bixby Bridge,
Big Sur*

Oatmeal Waffles

*Big Sur
Coastline*

The Windmill at
The Barnyard

Avocado & Cantaloupe Salad with Tangy Citrus Dressing

Carmel Mission
Courtyard

Monarchs in
Pacific Grove

Hot & Sour Prawns with Watercress

Pacific Grove
Victorian

Pacific Grove Victorian

Banana Cake

Lover's Point, Pacific Grove

Banana Cake

1/2 pound sweet butter
1 cup granulated sugar
2 eggs
1 cup mashed ripe
    bananas
1 3/4 cups unbleached all
    purpose flour
1/2 teaspoon salt
2/3 teaspoon baking soda

5 tablespoons buttermilk
1 teaspoon vanilla extract
1 1/2 to 2 medium
    size, firm but ripe
    bananas, sliced
1 1/2 cups shelled
    chopped walnuts
powdered sugar for
    dusting cake

Cream Cheese Frosting

8 ounces cream cheese, at
*   room temperature*
6 tablespoons sweet
*   butter, at room*
*   temperature*
3 cups powdered sugar
1 teaspoon vanilla extract
juice of 1/2 lemon

Preheat oven to 350°. Grease and flour 2 9-inch layer cake pans. Cream butter and sugar together. Add eggs, one at a time, beating well after each addition. Add mashed bananas, mixing thoroughly. Sift dry ingredients and add to butter and egg mixture. Stir until flour has been incorporated completely. Add buttermilk and vanilla. Mix for 1 minute. Pour batter into prepared pans. Set on the middle rack of the oven and bake at 350° for 25 to 30 minutes or until cake tester inserted into the center comes out clean. Cool in pans on rack for 10 minutes. Unmold and cool for 2 hours.

To prepare cream cheese frosting, cream together cream cheese and butter in mixing bowl. Add vanilla extract and lemon juice. Gradually add powdered sugar and mix until smooth.

When the cakes are cooled, place one layer on a serving plate and frost with cream cheese frosting. Arrange slices of banana over frosting. Cover with second layer and frost top and sides of the cake. Cover sides and top with chopped nuts. Dust the top of the cake with powdered sugar.

Serves eight to ten.

Chocolate Zucchini Cake

1/2 cup butter, at room temperature
1/2 cup oil
1 3/4 cups sugar
2 eggs
1 teaspoon vanilla
1/2 cup buttermilk or sour milk
2 1/2 cups flour
1/4 cup cocoa
1 teaspoon baking soda
1 teaspoon baking powder
1/2 teaspoon salt
1/2 teaspoon cinnamon
1/2 teaspoon cloves
1/4 cup chopped pecans
2 cups grated zucchini
1/2 cup chocolate chips
1/2 cup powdered sugar

Preheat oven to 325°. Cream together butter, oil and sugar. Beat in eggs, vanilla and buttermilk. Sift dry ingredients together. Combine wet and dry ingredients. Fold chopped pecans, zucchini, and chocolate chips into batter. Pour batter into 9x13x2 inch lightly greased pan. Bake at 325° for 40 to 45 minutes. Remove from oven and sprinkle with powdered sugar.

Serves ten.

Yogurt Poppy Seed Cake

1 cup vanilla yogurt
1/2 cup poppy seeds
1 cup whole milk
1 1/2 cups butter
(3 sticks)
1 1/2 cups sugar
4 large eggs
2 tablespoons vanilla
3 1/2 cups flour
1/4 teaspoon salt
1 tablespoon baking soda

Preheat oven to 350°. Mix yogurt, poppy seeds and milk together and let stand overnight, covered.

Cream together butter and sugar. Add eggs and vanilla. Sift dry ingredients together. Add flour mixture and yogurt-poppy seed mixture alternately to creamed ingredients. Spoon batter into tube or loaf pan, greased and dusted with flour, and bake at 350° until it tests done, approximately 50 minutes. Remove from pan after 10 minutes. Very moist. Stores well and can be frozen.

Serves ten to twelve.

*C*armelites still struggle to keep a sense of community in the village, now populated with more tourists than year-round residents. One way is through the daily trek to the post office, a journey that is both traditional and mandatory.

As with most small towns, all mail in the early days of Carmel was delivered to a central post office where residents would greet each other while perusing the day's letters. When the postal service offered to provide door to door delivery if the houses in the city were numbered, the Carmel population revolted and the city council passed an ordinance barring houses from posting addresses.

The fire department, on the other hand, needed to know the exact location of each house, so residents signify their homes by naming them.

Enchanting Dusted Almond Cake

Strong winter storms threatened to wash Ocean Avenue downhill into the Pacific Ocean, and the street was known as "the devil's staircase" because of the many potholes. Wooden sidewalks kept residents out of the dirt and muck when strolling the street.

After the city incorporated in 1916, the city council planned to pave the street, but the artist community, afraid their refuge would become too commercialized, sued the city fathers and won on a technicality. They danced in the dirt streets to celebrate their victory.

When Ocean Avenue was finally paved in 1922, the city government, now under the sway of the preservationists, hired a planner to route all automobiles out of the center of town. That was too much for the Carmel businessmen, who revolted and voted the city council out of office.

❦

Cake
4 ounces unsalted butter
8 ounces almond paste
  (not Marzipan)
3/4 cup granulated sugar
3 eggs, room temperature
1/2 teaspoon almond
  extract
1 tablespoon orange
  liqueur
1/4 cup all purpose flour
1/3 teaspoon baking
  powder

Raspberry Coulis
1 package frozen
  raspberries, thawed
2 to 3 tablespoons
  Framboise or other
  raspberry liqueur

Preheat oven to 350°. Cake: Cream butter, almond paste and sugar. Beat in eggs one at a time. Add almond extract and liqueur. Mix well. Add flour and baking powder mixing only until blended. (Do not overbeat.) Pour batter into a buttered and floured 8 inch round cake pan. Bake at 350° for 35 minutes or until cake tester comes out clean when inserted. When cool invert onto platter and dust with powdered sugar. Freezes well. Keeps for 3-4 days.

Raspberry Coulis: Puree frozen raspberries in blender. Push through a strainer to remove seeds. Add Framboise or liqueur to taste. Put spoonful of sauce on plate, add slice of cake and garnish with mint leaves and fresh raspberries.

Serves eight.

❦

Cream Cheese Pound Cake

Pound Cake
1 1/2 cups butter
   (3 sticks), at room
   temperature
8 ounces cream cheese,
   at room temperature
3 cups cake flour, sifted
3 cups sugar, sifted
1 1/2 teaspoons vanilla
   extract
6 eggs, lightly beaten

*Hot Spiced
   Blueberry Sauce*
1 cup fresh blueberries
   (frozen may be used)
1/2 teaspoon cinnamon
1/4 teaspoon ground
   nutmeg
1/4-1/2 cup sugar

Mix butter and cream cheese together. Add remaining ingredients and mix well. Pour mixture into greased and floured tube or bundt pan. START IN COLD OVEN. Bake at 300° for 1 1/2 hours. Never fails, always moist, easy to prepare. Serve alone or with the blueberry sauce over it.

Blueberry Sauce: Combine ingredients in a pan over medium heat. Bring to a boil. Boil 5 minutes, stirring occasionally.

Mocha Crunch Ice Cream Cake

Sauce
1 1/2 cup water
1/2 cup sugar
2 1/2 tablespoons instant
   espresso powder
12 ounces semi sweet
   chocolate, chopped
   (or use chips)
6 tablespoons unsalted
   butter

Crust
3 cups macaroon
   cookie crumbs
   (approximately 21
   Mothers cookies,
   crumbled)
1/2 cup unsalted butter

Filling
2 pints chocolate
   ice cream
2 pints coffee ice cream
3/4 cup chopped
   Heath Bars

Heat water, sugar and espresso powder in heavy saucepan over low heat until sugar dissolves. Add chocolate and butter. Stir until melted. Cool completely.

Grease 9-inch springform pan. Mix 2 cups crumbs with melted butter. Press firmly into pan bottom. Freeze. Soften chocolate ice cream and spread over crust. Freeze. Spoon 1/2 cup chocolate sauce over chocolate ice cream and sprinkle with remaining cup of crumbs. Freeze until firm. Soften coffee ice cream and spread over previous layer. Spread 1/2 cup sauce on top and sprinkle chopped Heath bars on top. Freeze until firm.

Serves eight.

Saronno Zuccotto

1 10-3/4-ounce frozen
    pound cake, thawed,
    sliced 1/4" thick
1/4 cup Amaretto or
    Kahlua, or more
    as needed
2 cups heavy cream
1/2 cup chopped pecans
1/2 cup sliced almonds
1/2 cup chocolate
    mini-chips
1/2 cup chocolate chips,
    melted

Toast pecans and almonds in 350° oven.

Line a 1 1/2 quart round bowl or loaf pan with damp cheese cloth or foil. Cut foil large enough so there is an overhang over the side of the bowl or pan. Cut cake slices in half to make triangles. Line pan with slices. Sprinkle liqueur over cake. Whip cream until very stiff. Using half of the whipped cream, mix in pecans, almonds and mini-chips. Spread in cake lined pan half-way up. Chill. Mix melted chocolate into remaining whipped cream, pour into pan on top of nuts and chips mixture. Cover with remaining cake slices and sprinkle with liqueur. Cover with foil or cheesecloth and chill overnight. Uncover and use cheesecloth or foil overhang to pull cake out of bowl and invert on plate. Decorate with whipped cream rosettes, sliced almonds and candied cherries.

It's beautiful, easy and delicious.

Serves six to eight.

One of the yearly highlights on Carmel Beach is the Great Sand Castle Contest. Always held on a Sunday, the date fluctuates and is only announced a few days ahead. It is usually in October, or as one sponsor put it, "It's held on the first Sunday after school opens and when the tide will be out from 11 to 5 and when there hasn't been too much publicity."

The local chapter of the American Institute of Architects sponsors the event, announces the yearly theme, and provides judges and prizes. Bribery, especially with food and drink, is highly encouraged by the judges, and serious builders come complete with coolers and barbecue grills to sustain the sculptors and con the critics. Prizes are given in many categories, but the most coveted of all is the Golden Shovel Award. Children are encouraged to join in the fun and all receive a special participatory plaque.

Bread Pudding with Brandy Sauce

Bread Pudding
3 eggs, lightly beaten
3/4 cup sugar
3 cups milk
1 cup whipping cream
1/2 cup margarine or
    butter, melted
1 tablespoon vanilla
1 teaspoon nutmeg
1/2 cup raisins
8 slices of stale French
    bread, cut 1/2
    inch thick

Brandy Sauce
1/2 cup sugar
1/2 cup unsalted butter
1 1/2 tablespoons milk
1 egg, beaten
1/4 cup brandy, or to
    taste

To prepare Bread Pudding: Mix together all ingredients except the bread. Put bread pieces in large bowl. Pour the egg mixture over the bread slices and let sit 20 minutes. Lightly grease a 4 quart baking dish, and place bread slices in it. If there is any egg mixture left, pour it over the bread. Bake, uncovered, 45 minutes or until the custard is set and the top is slightly browned.

To prepare Brandy Sauce: In medium saucepan, cook over low heat the sugar, butter and milk until the sugar dissolves. Cool 5 minutes. Stir in beaten egg and liquor to taste. Serve over warm or room temperature bread pudding.

Serves four.

Benefactors & Patrons

Cookbook Development Committee

Martha Doherty
Katee Leach

1992-1994

Maria Anderson
Suzanne Case
Lynn Clements
Sandra Kasky
Donna Wagnon

1993-1994

Janice McFarlane
Kathy Pomeroy
Jackie Reeves
Bonnie Huntington
   Vogel
Susan Warmington

1992-1993

Dottie Bradbury
Kathryn Cadigan
Terri Carlson
Betsy Cleary

The Junior League of Monterey County, Inc. would like to thank the following benefactors and patrons for supporting their community by making Feast of Eden *possible.*

Benefactors

Janie L. Kaufman

Nancy J. Rembert

Hanson, Rotter, Green
   CPAs

Louise Guard

Richard and Janis Outten

Lynn B. Storey

Patrons

Maria Anderson
Paula Beckman
Rosemary Bello
Roberta Bialek
Mary B. Bower
Patricia H. Brandt
Kathleen Burke
Virginia Carey
Carol Champlin
Patricia Tynan Chapman
Cecile R. Cranston
Carolyn Crockett
Claire Shoff Davis
Karen Day
Maryn and Derek
   Derdivanis
Gloria Didion
Jean L. Draper
Patricia Felix
Marilyn B. Flannery
April and Daniel Green

Janice L. Gryp
Ksenija Halamandaris
Nancy Eccles Hayward
Bridget M. Hildebrand
Mrs. Christopher Hillard
Peggy Johnsen
Sandra Kasky
Charles Keller
Marilyn Kren
Lamar Brothers Tire
   Service Inc.
Mary Ann Lawson
Catherine J. Lee
Mrs. Duncan Lewis
Harriet Sperry MacAlpine
Paula and Tom Mallett
Julie A. Matuszek
Patty McAffee
Janice McFarlane
Jackie Menke
Jean B. Mitchell
Mrs. Clifford Mettler
Anita Muhs
Dorthea Mumford
Nancy Newell
Katie Patterson
Barbara M. Porter
Cherie Robertson
Betty Roome
Mary Louise Schneeberger
Mary Shaw
Elizabeth A. Skou
Vicki Stewart
Diane M. Sweet
Jean Lapham Thomas
Joann Vaughan
Suzanne von Drachenfels
Karen Watkins
Beverly Moore Weakely
Patricia S. Work
Michelle Zimmerman

Contributors

Maly Adams
Annette Alcocer
Charlotte Allen
Mary May Altenburg
Barbara Antonacci
Jacqueline Armstrong
Paula Arnold
Yvonne Ascher
Sherrill Ash
Janell Ashing
Anne S. Ast
Virginia Atkinson
Judy B. Attwell
Susan Aucutt
Diane Ausonio
Bargetto Winery
Doug Barton
Gerald Barton
Jo Barton
Laurie Benjamin
Bernardus Winery
Patty Blurton
Hetty Bock
Patti Boitano
Susan Bollinger
Helen Booth
Mary Bower
Berenice Brattain
Mary Brinton
Susie Brusa
Wendy Brodie
Fritzi Broers
Mary Buckley
Ellyse Burke
Kathleen Burke
Alison Burleigh
Mindy Bush
Dawn Byram
Tim Cadigan
Eunice Campbell
Sally Cantor
Virginia Carey
Betty Case

Cheryl Cates
Katherine Caves
Luanne Caylor
Carol Champlin
Denise Chapman
Patricia Chapman
Michelle Comeau
Mary Conroy
Alvina Corvello
Jan Covell
Carolyn Craig
Jean Craig
Anne Crisan
Yvonne Cronin
Jerian Crosby
Meridith Crowell
Janet Crowley
Anne Lew D'Amico
Gloria Dake
Deidre Darst
Claire Davis
Karen Day
Heather Deming
Gloria Didion
Anne Dobler
Fred Doherty
Joan Downey
Mimi Drummond
Cheryl Duffus
Gigi Eastman
Barb Egland
Barbara Eklund
Sally Eldredge
Madonna Engle
Nancy Erdbacher
Lynn Flannery
Harriet Freeman
Marigrace Eldredge
  Gamble
Jeanne Gibson
Zac Gibson

(Continued on next page)

*Cookbook Proposal
Committee 1991-1992*

Gloria Dougherty
Claudia McCord

Roberta Atkinson
Terri Carlson
Carolyn Crockett
Maryn Pitt Derdivanis
Debra Kaczmar
Carolyn Rose
Debra Udycz

*Cookbook Research
Committee 1989-1991*

Carolyn Humphreys

Nancy Canning
Maryn Pitt Derdivanis
Gloria Dougherty
Debra Kaczmar
Katee Leach
Kelly Oard
Carolyn Rose

Kim Gill
Pat Gillooly
Vearl Goode
April Green
Jan Gryp
Brenda Guy
Glen Hammer
Karen Handley
Dorthy Hansen
Richard Hansen
Carolyn Hardy
Joan Harris
Chris Haupt
Martha Hawley
Shirley Hayward
Sue Hebert
Jean Herbold
Sue Hillard
Cynthia Holley
Lisa Hollo
Susan Hovde
Sherry Hove
Roberta Huntington
Ann Hutchinson
Nancy Hutchinson
Karen Juhring
Jon Kasky
Janie Kaufman
Noel Kelsh
Judith Kennedy
Julie Kennedy
Juliana Kierstead
Mark Killeen
Virginia Kinninger
Angelica Kocek
Carol Kolb
Donna Kolb
Earl Kolb
Teresa Kraft
Marilyn Kren
Beth Kurzava
Mollie Langhout
Kathi Lares
Don Leach
Cathy Lee
Dianne Le Lout
Elizabeth Lindsey
Allison Livesay

Sue Lloyd-Finlen
Lockwood Vineyards
Rita Lopez
Elizabeth Lord
Zo Lord
Harriet MacAlpine
Junita Mah
Paula Mallet
Bea Matthews
Bea McCord
Barbara McGowan
Jennifer McNamara
Barbara Menhinick
Patricia Mettler
Dorothy Middaugh
Barbara Mikolasko
Nancy Miller
Eleanor Mitchell
Hildegarde Mitchell
Jean Mitchell
Nancy Modrall
Liz Monroe
May Montgomery
Jann Moreland
Anne Morton
Dianne Mouisset
Anita Muhs
Mimi Muhs
Deborah Nelson
Stephanie Nelson
Kathy Newell
Phyllis Nicholas
Melanie Nicora
Michelle Noseworthy
Jan Nutton
Karin Oliver
Julie Ostarello
Lisa Ostarello
Janis Bass Outten
Sandi Pappani
Paraiso Springs Vineyards
Erin Parkhurst
Katharine Patterson
Betsey Pearson
Jane Pelletier
Gail Pieper

(Continued on next page)

Cheryl Pisto
Gia Pisto
Jeanette Pruin
Nancy Quackenbush
Gloria Quequep
Patti Ramos
Missy Read
Nancy Rembert
Paul Rembert
Mary Rice
Beverly Ridley
Dee Robertson
Esther Rodriguez
Gerta Rohrs
John Romano
Madeline Ross
Benita Rumold
Joanne Rush
Lynn Santos
Julie Satow
Debra Schadeck
Robin Schafer
Cynthia Schelcher
Cathy Scherzer
Kim Schott
Mary Schrady
Lynda Schraegle
Anne Scoville
Kristin Searle
Renata Seme
Mary Shaw
Jan Shearer
Connie Chedester Smith
Kathryn Sparolini
Pauline Stanley
Virginia Stanton
Paula Stark
Freida Steiner
Valerie Steiney
Sara Stevens
Vicki Stewart
Dianne Stracuzzi
Danna Sharp Stringer
Gloria Struve
Lorene Sublett
Liz Sugar
David Swede
Margaret Swede

Jennifer Sylverstein
Janice Tancredi
Elizabeth Taylor
Lesile Taylor
Lynne Temple
Jean Thomas
Wendy Thomas
Burney Threadgill
P. Timm
Diana Trapani
Bob Tripp
Jan Tripp
Karen Vandergrift
Joann Vaughan
Ventanna Vineyards
Lois Lagier Verga
Barbara Walcom
Melissa Walker
Gayle Walsh
Lora Warren
Peggy Warren
Cam Watkins
Karen Watkins
Elizabeth Watt
Edward Wilson
Susan Wilson
Emily Woudenberg
Michelle Zimmerman

and special thanks to
Debbie Etienne

Index

Order Form

To order additional copies, please send this form with payment to:

Feast of Eden
P.O. Box 2291
Monterey, CA 93942-2291

No. of copies _____ @ $19.95 ea.	
Postage & handling**	
Sales tax (California residents) @ $ 1.45 ea.	
TOTAL	

Postage & handling
up to $21.50: $3.50
$21.50 - $43.50: $4.00
$43.00 - $65.00: $4.50
$65.00 - $86.00: $5.00
$86.00 - $130.00: $6.00

Name_____

Address_____

City_____ State_____ Zip_____

Make checks payable to:
The Junior League of Montery County, Inc.

Please charge to my   Visa ☐   Mastercard ☐

Card number _____

Exp. date_____

Name on card_____

Signature_____

Gift wrap and send to the following:

Name_____

Address_____

City_____ State_____ Zip_____

Please allow 2-3 weeks for delivery. Please call for information regarding one or two day delivery. International delivery is available. Please call for further information. Tel: 408-345-1103
Fax: 408-375-3739